Daytime
LIVE

GARDENING
BOOK

GARDENING BOOK

Practical Advice from
Daytime Live's
Gardening Expert
ALAN TITCHMARSH

BBC BOOKS

Picture credits

All the photographs are © Alan Titchmarsh
except for the colour photograph of the
millstone fountain at the Chelsea Flower
Show which is © Michael Warren and the
photograph on page 44 of Jilly Cooper which
is © Peter Woloszynski.

The drawings are by Marilyn Leader.

Published by BBC Books
a division of BBC Enterprises Limited
Woodlands, 80 Wood Lane, London W12 0TT

© Alan Titchmarsh 1989

ISBN 0 563 20761 2

Set in 9 on 10 pt Esprit by Ace Filmsetting Ltd, Frome, Somerset
Cover printed by Richard Clay Ltd, Norwich, Norfolk
Printed and bound by Richard Clay Ltd, Bungay & Norwich

CONTENTS

INTRODUCTION

'You make it all sound so simple,' said the lady in her letter. It's the best compliment I've ever had. You see, as far as I'm concerned, gardening is about enjoyment. I know that there are times when it's about frustration, worry, irritation, annoyance, desperation and cluelessness, but basically it's about common sense and fun, and I've never seen any point in pretending anything else.

Some folk can make the simplest job sound complicated, so I've always tried, on television, to be clear and practical and a bit of a giggle as well.

Most Fridays on *Daytime Live* (weather and producers permitting), I'm given anything from five to eight minutes to inspire the nation's gardeners to green up the land around them. It might be making a window-box, potting up house plants or visiting some famous celebrity to see how his or her garden grows. But whatever the subject, it has to be crammed into that pint pot with clarity and without looking too rushed or confusing. Sometimes I win, and sometimes I lose, but either way the mailbag continues to bulge with problem letters.

I get rotting leaves from all corners of Britain (and a few from Europe, too). There are garden plans drawn on Basildon Bond with pleas for suggested plants for the difficult places. And there are always requests for cures for ground elder, bindweed and couch grass.

Here, then, is the answer to at least a few of your problems. The *Daytime Live Gardening Book* will tell you just what to do with your ground elder, how to start out on a new patch of ground, and how to enjoy your garden. With any luck it will also leave you with enough time to watch a spot of television.

STARTING FROM SCRATCH

Gazing out on to a sea of mud, rough grass, builders' rubble and puddles in clay is not guaranteed to inspire anyone who has a new garden. It's more likely to put them off for life. But tackle the job slowly and methodically and you'll feel you're getting somewhere.

The patch of garden you look at most is that right outside the kitchen window, especially if the sink looks out on to it. Start there. Clear away rubble, fork over the ground and pull out thick weed roots. Don't put them on the compost heap (see page 11) where they'll probably survive, but drop them into black plastic bin liners and take them to the local dump.

There's a great temptation to rush for the weedkiller in these circumstances, but as all your soil will have to be dug or forked over at least once when your garden is being made, I've always thought that such applications are rather pointless.

Don't do too much at once. Fifteen minutes' digging a day is ample to start with. You can build up to half an hour or even an hour after a week or two.

The reason why we dig (and on heavy soil a fork is often much easier to use than a spade) is to relieve compaction, improve drainage, make it possible to remove weed roots and to work in garden compost or well-rotted manure – the bulky organic matter that really improves soil. When you first dig your garden there's no finer way of improving your soil than digging in this stuff (see pages 10 and 11).

That little patch of ground outside the kitchen window can be planted up with spring or summer bedding plants to give you instant colour while you go about planning the way the rest of the garden will look.

Some experts suggest planning your garden on squared paper. If you're a natural draughtsman, go ahead. I'm not, and I find it much easier to go upstairs and look out of the bedroom window. From there I can direct another member of the family to make trails of sand to mark out beds and borders, and bamboo canes are stuck in for trees and shrubs.

If you've inherited an established garden but want to make changes, wait for a year before digging up beds and borders. By then you'll have seen what comes up, and you can decide what to keep and what to ditch. It's a great excuse for taking your time.

You can plant new shrubs at their final spacings to allow for growth, and fill in between them until they reach their maximum size with annual bedding plants. Alternatively, you can plant them rather closer together with a view to removing one or two at a later date when overcrowding occurs. I always opt for the latter, being a bit impatient. That way you can keep the best shrubs and dispense with the services of those which fail to thrive or don't please you.

Soil is not a pretty thing and I see no point in keeping it in public view. It simply acts as a breeding ground for weeds, and the constant hoeing needed to keep them down can result in damage to the roots of shrubs and cause roses, for instance, to produce suckers. Keep your ground covered with plant foliage and not only are the weeds squeezed out but the canopy also helps to retain moisture and make for better growth of the plants themselves.

There's no magic way of making an instant garden. Take everything slowly and steadily and enjoy your leisurely progress.

8

THE BASIC TOOL-SHED

You don't need to surround yourself with a vast battery of offensive weapons in the gardening game. A few well-chosen pieces will enable you to cope with ease. Hardware shops and garden centres display dozens of different implements. Choose those that are well made and comfortable to handle. Here's my selection of essentials:

Spade

Choose one with a 'Y'-shaped handle; it's less blister-making than a 'T'-shape. Make sure that the junction between wooden shaft and steel socket is smooth. If a standard-sized spade is too heavy, choose a border spade, which is smaller.
Use for: digging soil, planting trees and shrubs, slicing up clumps of border perennials to propagate by division in autumn and spring.

Fork

As for the spade. I find that the border fork is the most frequently used gardening tool in my shed.
Use for: pricking over soil between established plants, working in fertiliser, breaking down rough-dug soil, digging heavy soil where a spade is difficult to use, moving compost and manure, spiking the lawn to improve drainage.

Rake

If possible, choose one with a smooth, light, alloy shaft. The head should be one entire casting – not nails piercing a flattened piece of steel.
Use for: levelling cultivated soil (never over-rake – it leads to crustiness of the soil surface), clearing leaves, taking out and filling in seed drills, earthing up potatoes and celery.

Dutch hoe

The best weeder in the garden. Keep it sharpened with a file so that it severs annual weeds from their roots. The shaft should be smooth and the head not too heavy.
Use for: killing weeds (skim it over the surface – don't push it too deeply into the soil), taking out seed drills (use the corner pulled against a taut garden line).

Trowel

Make sure the blade and stalk are firmly welded together and that the stalk is securely attached to the handle. The top of the handle should be smooth so that it can sit in the palm of the hand with comfort. Stainless steel trowels are especially easy to use.
Use for: planting bulbs, bedding plants and perennials.

Secateurs

The one piece of equipment worth splashing out on. Felco secateurs are not cheap but are guaranteed for life and are sharp and extremely comfortable to use.
Use for: pruning any stem up to finger-thickness.

Shears

Choose a light pair which have good rubber buffers to take the jarring out of the cutting action. The blades should slice cleanly against one another. Keep them free of dried sap by rubbing them with wet emery paper after use.
Use for: hedge clipping, grass clipping, lightly snipping over heathers after flowering.

These essentials, plus a mower (see page 20) and a wheelbarrow will serve you well.

YOUR SOIL

You'll only get out of soil what you put into it. It's the most boring-looking stuff on earth but it doesn't half make plants grow if it's beefed up with garden compost or well-rotted animal manure.

The 'well-rotted' bit is important. Dig in fresh manure or compost and the bacteria in the soil will have to work so hard to break it down that they'll use up that valuable plant food nitrogen. You may not notice it, but your plants will and their growth will slow down and their leaves become yellow.

When you first dig over your soil, add manure or compost at around a bucketful to the square yard (sq m) – more if you can spare it. Bulky organic matter like this helps to improve drainage and adds nutrition, too. You can choose all sorts of bulky soil improvers that are as good for sandy soils as for clay:

Peat is only as good as it feels. It contains no nutrients. It is also rather expensive.

Well-rotted manure is wonderful – bulky and nutritious.

Garden compost is nearly as rich as manure.

Spent mushroom compost is well-rotted manure plus chalk (and a few mushrooms). Nutritious and easy to handle.

Leafmould is rotted leaves. Good for bulk but not much nutrition.

Sharp grit is not organic but it's great at improving clay soil. Dig it in with manure or compost; it lasts well.

Plants also need three main foods: nitrogen (N), phosphates (P) and potash (K), which are all contained in a general fertiliser such as blood, bone and fishmeal. Apply this in early spring at the rate of a couple of clenched fistfuls to the square yard (sq m). Lightly hoe or fork it in.

Growmore contains the same nutrients but is inorganic and does nothing for soil life. Bacteria are needed to break down the organic blood, bone and fishmeal and so are kept in employment. I reckon that's vital.

Blood, bone and fishmeal should be your main fertiliser. Apply it every spring. You can also use sulphate of ammonia *very* sparingly to give plants that refuse to grow a kick in the pants. Apply one clenched fistful to each shrub, or two to a tree in early spring. It contains oodles of nitrogen and promotes leaf and shoot growth.

Anything in the garden that refuses to flower can be given rose fertiliser (high in flower-promoting potash), and anything in pots that refuses to flower can be watered at 10-day intervals with dilute liquid tomato food. It works wonders!

Lime

No, don't switch off. This complicated subject is really not difficult to master. Simple soil-testing kits can be bought and will show you how acid or alkaline (limy) your soil is. Limy or chalky soil won't grow rhododendrons, azaleas, camellias, many heathers, pieris and other lime-hating shrubs. There's nothing you can do about this. Just enjoy the wide range of plants that you *can* grow.

Acid soil (without any lime or chalk) will grow many plants (including rhododendrons and the like) but some vegetables will not enjoy it. That's why lime is often applied to vegetable plots in winter, but it should never be applied at the same time as manure – the two interact badly.

THE COMPOST HEAP

Mystery surrounds the compost heap, but it's really just a simple means of making your own manure. Every garden should have two.

Make them side by side. Two post-and-wire enclosures 3 or 4 feet (90 or 120 cm) square mean that while one is full and rotting, the other is being filled. With just one heap the whole business becomes confusing and messy.

Make both fronts removable so that the finished compost can be easily extracted.

What goes in? All annual weeds, vegetable waste, lawn mowings, cabbage leaves, potato peelings, tea-leaves, coffee grounds, pea pods, crushed eggshells and soft prunings.

What stays out? Thick-rooted perennial weeds and woody stems. Household food (because there is the risk of encouraging rats and mice).

So far, so good, but how do you make it all turn brown? The answer is to mix all your ingredients together so that there's no concentration of one thing in one place. Firm the heap regularly by trampling. Turn a hose on it at the first sign of dryness, and throw a piece of old carpet or sacking over the top to keep in moisture.

Over every 9-inch (23-cm) layer, add a sprinkling of garden soil and a couple of handfuls of sulphate of ammonia or a proprietary compost accelerator. There's no need to turn the heap at intervals, provided everything is mixed up when it's put in.

Three to six months later (the cooler the weather, the slower the rotting) you'll be able to dig out brown and crumbly goodness and dig it in or spread it on your soil. You will notice the difference in plant growth.

CROSS-SECTION OF COMPOST HEAP

1 *carpet or sacking*

2 *post*

3 *activator*

4 *greenstuff*

5 *full heap – rotting*

6 *wire netting enclosure*

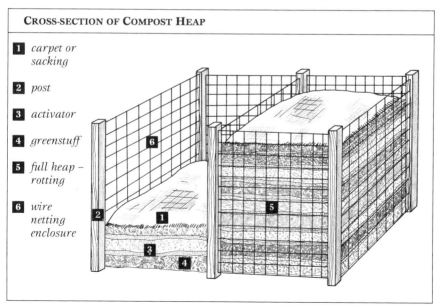

THE DESIGNER GARDEN

A fitted kitchen is a chef's idea of heaven. A fitted garden is a lazy gardener's dream. But why shouldn't it be a reality? It *is* possible to have a fitted 'designer garden' for less than the price of a fitted kitchen, as we proved on *Daytime Live* when we invited landscape gardener Bill Wrighton to design and fit our 'instant garden'.

We made several stipulations: the garden had to be a typically small plot like that found behind many houses. It had to cope with adults and small children, offering the children somewhere to play, and the adults somewhere to relax. It had to be designed for a relatively modest budget, and it had to look good all the year round.

Bill came up with a solution that turned our dream into reality. The garden is now just two years old, but already it looks decidedly mature.

Marking out

The garden plan should be transferred from paper to soil by using pegs and string so you can see exactly what goes where. Make any adjustments at this stage. Paths, lawn and patio areas should all be clearly indicated. Don't worry about showing the position of plants at this stage.

Tools needed: shovel, spade, fork, pick-axe, rammer, wheelbarrow, spirit level, level board, nylon line, pegs, trowel, lump hammer.

Mixtures

Mortar mix – 4 parts building sand, 1 part cement plus water.
Dry mix – 5 parts building sand, 1 part cement, no water.
Concrete – 4 parts gravel, 2 parts concreting sand, 1 part cement, plus water.

Hardcore – rubble such as broken bricks or slabs.
Mixing – place sand/gravel on flat surface and sprinkle cement over top. Mix thoroughly. Make a hole in the centre and add water. Mix, adding more water as needed to make a stiff consistency.
Laying surface – fine ash or sand.

Laying hard surfaces

Mark out the areas using pegs, spirit level and board and fasten lines to the pegs to indicate finished slab or brick level. Alongside the house, this level should be two courses of bricks below damp-proof course level.

There should be a 6-inch (15-cm) gap between the level of the string and the surface of the soil. Dig out soil if necessary.

Place 4 inches (10 cm) of hardcore over the area to be slabbed, and ram it firm. Cover it with a thin layer of ash or sand. The surface should be firm and level.

Slabs can be laid on five generous spots of mortar and tamped into position with the handle of the lump hammer. Make sure the surface of each slab runs true to the line. Butt the slabs up against one another, staggering the joints. Fitted close together like this, square-edged slabs need no grouting.

Bevel-edged slabs, which have a more natural look, should be laid on loose-levelled dry mix and tamped down until level with the line. The joints, ½ inch (1–1.5 cm) wide, should be filled with dry mix.

Brick pavers are laid on 2-inch (5-cm) sharp sand over hardcore and firmed into place with a lump hammer knocked against a board. Edges may have to be mortared into position, and the gaps filled with fine, dry sand.

Timber work

Softwood or hardwood can be used, planed or sawn, and treated with timber preservative other than creosote which is toxic to plants.

Post holes should be between 1½ and 2 feet (45-60 cm) deep, and the base of each post should be set in concrete which is less likely to lead to rotting than when in soil.

Use non-rusting nails or screws.

Brickwork

Peg out the full extent of the brickwork and dig out footings 6 to 8 inches (15-20 cm) below surrounding levels and 3 inches (7.5 cm) wider than the bricks on both sides (that is, 6 inches (15 cm) wider than the finished wall).

Place concrete in the footings so that it is 4 to 6 inches (10-15 cm) deep and below the finished soil surface. You can lay bricks 24 hours after laying the concrete.

Start at the corners or ends of the wall and lay one brick at each extremity, checking that such bricks are on the same level as one another. Use a line stretched between them to make sure that all other bricks are at the same level.

Adjust the string to mark the level of each course as the wall rises. Scrape off surplus mortar as you proceed and, at the end of your work, use an old piece of copper tubing to run along all the joints. This rebates them slightly and gives a smart finish.

Lawns

Don't stint on the soil preparation and levelling, whether you are sowing seed or laying turf. See pages 18 and 19 for details.

Planting

Choose all your plants with great care. Check that their ultimate height and spread is something you can cope with, or be prepared to prune them drastically (something that can ruin a specimen shrub like a magnolia).

Check whether a plant is suited to sun or shade (see pages 56-59), and give thought to what it will look like alongside its neighbours.

Plant at spacings which will allow room for growth, but which will ensure good weed suppression and rapid impact. If you plant things relatively close together you can always dig up and move one or two when overcrowding occurs. That's far better than watching bare patches fill with weeds.

In general, small plants should be set at the front of borders and taller ones behind them. Make sure that a good few plants are evergreen – this will give the garden form all the year round.

Before planting, enrich the soil with compost or manure. Container-grown shrubs, trees and perennials can be planted at any time of year. Water them before planting and remove the pot immediately the hole has been dug. Each hole should be larger than the root-ball it is to take, and the soil should be firmed back with your welly once the plant is in position. When planted, the surface of the root-ball should rest just below the surface of the soil.

Trees will need a stake in their early years. Knock this into the hole before the tree is inserted and fasten the stem to the stake with proprietary tree ties, top and bottom. The top of the stake should finish well below the lowest branch. (See page 15.) Check the ties regularly to make sure they are not restricting the sap flow, and remove the stake after a couple of years.

Mulch your instant garden with something like pulverised or chipped bark. It may be pricy but it lasts for four or five years, shows off the plants well, keeps down weeds and keeps in moisture. Spread it 2 or 3 inches (5-7.5 cm) deep on the surface of clean, moist soil and watch it work for you.

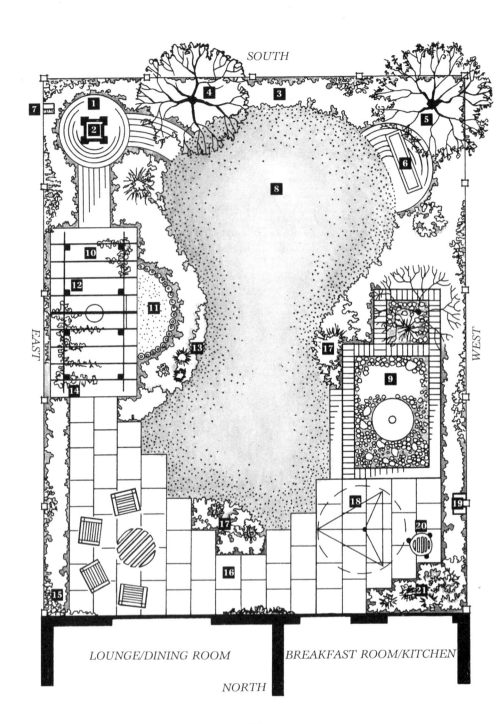

SOUTH

EAST

WEST

LOUNGE/DINING ROOM

BREAKFAST ROOM/KITCHEN

NORTH

14

DESIGNER GARDEN PLAN

1 Circle in block paving
2 Bird bath
3 Mixed shrubs for all-year interest
4 Gleditsia triacanthos 'Sunburst'
  (honey locust)
5 Betula jacquemontii (silver birch)
6 Bench seat
7 Bird box
8 Lawn
9 Water feature
10 Safety surface beneath (bark)
11 Sandpit with play logs
12 Timber pergola with play equipment
13 Heathers and conifers
14 Climbing plants
15 Fragrant climbing plant
  (honeysuckle)
16 Patio – riven-faced York paving
17 Winter colour
18 Rotary drier
19 Bird table
20 Barbecue
21 Herb garden

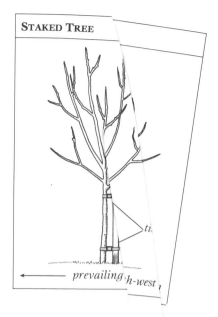

STAKED TREE

ti...

prevailing south-west ...

SECTION SHOWING WATER FEATURE

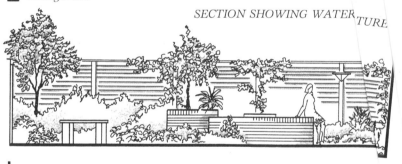

SECTION SHOWING TIMBER PERGOLA

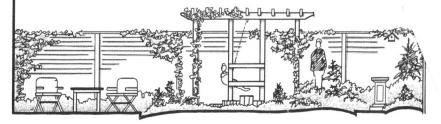

Not eve ne can run to a
design garden. When funds
are sh a way has to be found
to make a br t garden at the cost of
only a few nds.
Gardene are reat givers, and
you'll only ve t make it known in
your stree vill e that you're trying
to plant gar n for neighbours to
come ro wit cuttings of this and
clumps at.
But i u w to be self-sufficient,
nothin m cost effective than a
packe se Hardy annuals are
flow ed at can be sown in the
gard re where they are to grow.
Fro ly il the frosts they'll give
yo ill show, provided you give
th e ance to succeed.
time Live budget garden,
res just 15 feet by 20 feet
v m), we mapped out a St
ag pattern with bricks, and
iagonal stripes with gravel
had a border running round
e of the garden and four tri-
eds inside, divided by gravel

this pattern you can ring the
year after year, planting vege-
in the centre beds and flowers
the outside, or flowers in every
nd border.
mbers like sweet peas, runner
s and climbing nasturtiums can be
to hide the stark interwoven fenc-
that usually surrounds small gar-
ns, and they can also be trained up
igwams of bamboo canes in the cen-
ral beds to offer height.

Sowing the seeds
Fork over the soil during April, a week
or two before you sow. Work in a dusting of blood, bone and fishmeal – about
two handfuls to the square yard (sq m).

Immediately before you sow, rake the
soil level and mark out your 'drifts' of
each variety with trails of sand.

Press a bamboo cane flat against the
soil at 4-inch (10-cm) intervals within
each drift to make shallow drills, and
trickle the seeds of each variety quite
thinly into their allotted drills. Rake
back the soil. Large seeds like nasturtiums can be pushed in individually
with your fingers so that they are about
1 inch (2.5 cm) deep and 6 inches
(15 cm) apart.

Sweet pea seeds can be sown at the
foot of their wigwams of canes – two
seeds by each cane.

Cats can be a real problem when
they rake up newly cultivated soil. Lay
twiggy pea-sticks over the seed-beds
until the seedlings are well established.

Overcrowded seedlings should be
thinned out to leave one every 4 inches
(10 cm). The twiggy pea-sticks can be
pushed in among taller varieties to give
them support once they are 3 inches
(7.5 cm) high.

Sown in a sunny spot, and given
plenty of water in dry spells, your
hardy annuals will give you a smashing
show.

Try these: acroclinium, alyssum, baby
blue eyes (nemophila), baby's breath
(gypsophila), bartonia, calendula (pot
marigold), Californian bluebell
(phacelia), Californian poppy
(eschscholtzia), candytuft (iberis),
clarkia, corn-cockle (agrostemma),
annual cornflower, godetia, lavatera,
larkspur, love-in-a-mist (nigella),
mignonette, dwarf morning glory
(annual convolvulus – it's much better
than the weed!), nasturtium, poached
egg flower (limnanthes), rudbeckia,
night-scented and Virginian stocks.

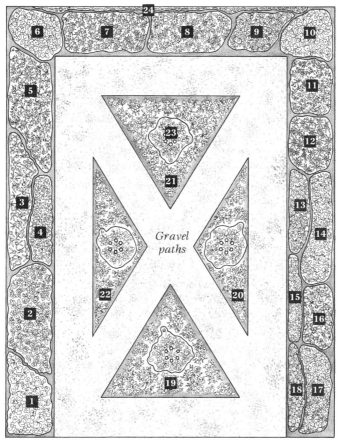

Gravel paths

1 Nasturtium 'Cherry Rose'	**13**	Candytuft
2 Clarkia (double mixed)	**14**	Agrostemma (corncockle)
3 Cornflower 'Diadem'	**15**	Night-scented stocks
4 Virginian stocks	**16**	Cornflower 'Diadem'
5 Larkspur	**17**	Eschscholzia mixed
6 Lavatera 'Silver Cup'	**18**	Alyssum
7 Dimorphotheca 'Glistening White'	**19**	Godetia 'Azalea Flowered'
8 Rudbeckia 'Marmalade'	**20**	Godetia 'Sybil Sherwood'
9 Limnanthes	**21**	Godetia 'Azalea Flowered'
10 Lavatera 'Mont Blanc'	**22**	Godetia 'Sybil Sherwood'
11 Larkspur	**23**	Runner beans up wigwam
12 Acroclinium	**24**	Sweet peas up fence

17

LAWNS

Even in small gardens a lawn seems to show everything off to perfection. Fair enough, in *very* small gardens it can be a headache if there's simply no room to turn round with a mower, and nowhere to put the clippings. In such cases a patio made of gravel or stone is a better bet – it's still sittable on but needs very little in the way of care and attention.

But when a lawn is decided upon, prepare yourself for a bit of hard graft. Whether seed or turf is chosen, the ground preparation is just the same. The soil needs to be dug or forked over and any rubble and perennial weed roots pulled out. Then the earth should be levelled with a rake and trampled firm with your feet. Rake it again, trample it again and rake once more, working in a couple of handfuls of blood, bone and fishmeal (yes, I know I use it for everything, but it works!). Then you're ready to sow or turf.

Springbok rake

Lawns from seed

Ten times cheaper than turf, a seed-raised lawn will be longer in establishing itself but just as good in the long run. Grass seed can be sown either in late April and early May, or in September. During autumn and winter it's too cold to sow, and in summer it's often too hot and dry (oh yes it is!).

Choose your grass seed mixture carefully. There are mixtures for very fine lawns which I wouldn't recommend unless you want to turn your lawn into an art form and cosset it every day. There are mixtures for shade (but not dense shade under trees where grass will refuse to grow), and there are mixtures containing rye-grasses which take wear and tear.

Choose a mixture containing dwarf rye-grasses and you'll get a good-looking, hard-wearing lawn. 'Hunter' rye-grasses are especially good.

Sow the seed at the rate of 1½ ounces to the square yard (50 g per sq m) (weigh the first lot and put it in an old yoghurt pot with a felt-tip mark on the side – use this as your measure). Scatter the seed evenly over each square yard (sq m), and when the entire area is sown, rake lightly to bury some of the seed.

Forget about bird deterrents. There's enough seed to let them have a nibble. Keep the soil moist when it shows signs of drying – turn on a lawn sprinkler. It will stop the birds taking dust baths.

When the grass is about 2 inches (5 cm) high, go over the lawn with a light roller, or the back roller of a lawnmower. The following day, mow the lawn, cutting off just the top ½ inch (1-1.5 cm) of grass.

Cut again when the lawn has grown a little more, and then begin your regu-

18

Laying turf

lar weekly mowing (if you've sown in late summer) or twice weekly (if you've sown in spring). Adjust the mower to cut a little closer each time until it is cutting the grass to about ¾ inch (2 cm).

Don't worry about the rash of annual weeds – mowing will soon kill them off.

Your seed-raised lawn will be ready to sit on in about eight weeks, but wait a little longer before using it as a football pitch.

Laying turf

Turfing produces the instant lawn, but at a price. Ground preparation is as for sowing grass seed. You can lay turf at any time of year provided the ground is neither muddy nor frozen, nor dust dry. Order turf from a reputable supplier. Many garden centres are now agents for a nationwide firm which specialises in growing different types of turf for different uses. This is far better than 'weed-treated meadow turf' so often sold for making lawns.

Order your turf and make sure it is scheduled to arrive when you are there to lay it. Turf stacked in rolls for more

than three or four days will rapidly turn yellow.

Lay one edge of the lawn, butting the turves closely together. Lay a plank across them and stand on it, working forwards from the row you've just laid. Bond the turves like bricks, staggering the joints and patting them into place with the back of a spade.

When the entire area has been covered, cut the edges to the required shape with a half-moon iron or with a spade.

Make sure a sprinkler is turned on in dry weather, and mow the lawn when it starts to grow.

Should the turf be allowed to dry out, it will shrink and turn strawy – keep the sprinkler handy!

LAWNS FOR THE LAZY

To make the idler's lawn, simply mow anything that grows on your patch of bare earth. Eventually you'll have a lawn, and after about five years you'll have a job to distinguish it from one that was sown or turfed!

MOWERS AND MOWING

There's always an argument about the best kind of lawnmower to use. The answer is to use the mower that does the kind of job that suits you. If you want a fine lawn, use a cylinder mower that collects the clippings. If you want stripes, the mower should have a large rear roller.

If you don't mind a slightly rougher lawn, use a rotary mower that collects the clippings. For larger areas of rough grass, choose a heavyweight rotary mower which needn't necessarily collect the clippings (but mow regularly so that they blow away rather than congregate in large clods).

If your lawn is steep or undulating, choose a hover mower for ease of use. That's all there is to it.

You can mow all the year round, weather permitting. Never cut too close; ½ inch (1-1.5 cm) at the absolute most; ¾ inch (2 cm) is better. Grass which is allowed to be ¾ inch (2 cm) long rather then ½ inch (1-1.5 cm) long will show much more resistance to drought in summer.

In summer cut twice a week. At other times of year cut to keep the lawn smart – as little as once a month will be enough.

LAWN CARE CALENDAR

January and February
Sweep off fallen leaves. Keep off the grass when it's frosty. Send the mower for servicing.

March
The lawn starts to grow in most years. Give it a light trim with the mower set high. Water on a moss-killer if moss is a problem, but remember that moss will return if the lawn is badly drained, shaded or poorly fed.

April
Mow more frequently. Rake out dead moss killed earlier. Trim lawn edges and re-cut those that are broken down.

May
Apply a combined weedkiller and fertiliser dressing with a wheeled distributor to make sure the application is even. Sow new lawns from seed.

June, July and August
Have the sprinkler handy in dry spells and leave it running for at least an hour in any one spot. (You'll need a sprinkler licence from your local water company.) Mow the lawn twice a week. Spot weedkiller can be used on stubborn weeds.

September
Start raising the cut of the mower. Apply an autumn lawn dressing. Later in the month, rake the grass with a wire-tooth 'springbok' rake. Spike the lawn with a fork and brush sharp sand into the holes. Sow lawns from seed, or lay turf.

October, November and December
Mowing frequency can be reduced and the height of cut raised. Lay turf in mild weather. Sweep off leaves and keep off the grass when it's frosted.

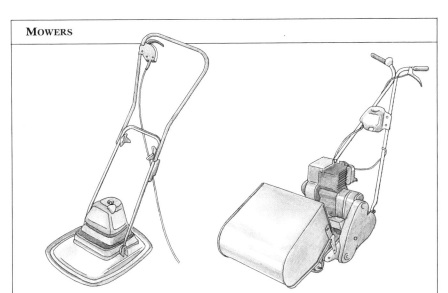

Hover Mower
Useful on steep banks and undulating ground, the hover mower rides on its own cushion of air

Cylinder Mower
This is the machine that produces the stripes – the only mower to use on a fine lawn

Rotary Mower
For coarser lawns and longer grass. Useful where the greensward is hard-wearing rather than of bowling-green standard

Strimmer
Use to cut long grass where mower cannot reach but take care to avoid damaging the bark around trees

BACKYARD GARDENING

Never complain about having a small garden. At least you know you can always keep up with it! Even the humble backyard with its forbidding walls or fences and its solid floor can be turned into a green oasis that's easy to look after, provided you remember that plants rely on you totally when it comes to food and water.

The backyard garden at *Daytime Live* is just that – a solid paved floor surrounded by a stone wall. But you can make variations on this theme.

Start by looking at the possibility of varying the texture of the floor. Brick pavers or paving slabs can be laid on a dry mortar or sand base (see pages 14–15), and other patches can be given over to gravel.

Washed pea shingle is by far the cheapest patio surface. Lay it directly on to firmed and weed-free ground, or on to black polythene stretched over the soil and perforated at intervals with a garden fork to allow rain to drain away. The polythene is extremely effective at preventing the re-emergence of weeds, but it can sometimes be exposed when the gravel is kicked around and then it doesn't look very nice. Either way, make your gravel between 1 inch (2.5 cm) and 1½ inches (4 cm) deep.

A few cobbles can be grouped together, and a hosta or other bold-leafed plant such as rodgersia or bamboo planted alongside them. Simply scrape away the gravel to plant, making a hole in the polythene if necessary.

If the floor of the backyard is simply earth, then spaces for beds and borders can be left when you are laying the hard surface. If the surface is hard from wall to wall, however, then you will have to rely totally on pots and tubs and

other containers to support your plants.

But you can cheat alongside walls. Build a dry wall with bricks to a height of three or four courses to create a free-standing trough at the foot of the backyard wall. Line the trough with old polythene sacks and fill it with John Innes No. 2 potting compost. Into this instant bed you can plant shrubs and perennials, annual bedding plants and bulbs. Even climbing plants will find enough sustenance in the compost and they can be trained up the wall to relieve that bare surface.

When it comes to persuading your climbers to leg it up the wall, look at the type of support systems they possess. Do they climb by means of twining stems (honeysuckle), sticky pads (Virginia creeper), tendrils (sweet peas), twining leaf stalks (clematis), aerial roots (ivy) or thorns (rambling rose)?

Those with aerial roots and sticky pads will cling to a wall or fence on their own. If they refuse, try painting the surface with manure water (half a bucket of manure, topped up with water and allowed to stand for a few days). Other climbers need a finer support system. Fasten horizontal wires to masonry nails knocked into the wall. A spacing of 18 inches (45 cm) between wires is about right. Alternatively, fasten wooden trelliswork to wooden battens attached to the wall and tie the stems in to this.

Whatever you use, this adaptable flower bed will make a great difference to your outlook right through the year. Start off with crocuses and dwarf narcissi (planted in autumn for a spring show) and go on to enjoy summer bedding (planted in late May). With a backbone of variegated evergreens like *Euonymus* 'Emerald 'n' Gold', a dwarf conifer or two with

8 feet (240 cm)

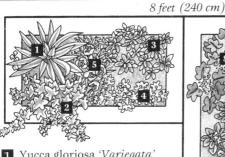

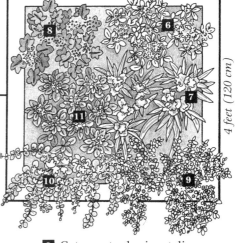

4 feet (120 cm)

1 Yucca gloriosa *'Variegata'*
(striped fountain of leaves)

2 *Variegated ivy*

3 *Euonymus 'Emerald 'n' Gold'*
(yellow and green evergreen
shrub)

4 Artemisia glacialis
(silver-grey ground hugger)

5 *Cobbles/gravel interplanted with*
crocuses

6 *Choisya 'Sundance'*
(yellow evergreen)

7 Iris pallida *'Aurea Variegata'*
(yellow and green striped
foliage)

8 *Heuchera 'Palace Purple'*
(purple sycamore-shaped leaves)

9 Cotoneaster horizontalis
'Variegata' (variegated
fishbone cotoneaster)

10 Lysimachia nummularia
'Aurea'
(golden-leafed creeping jenny)

11 Ajuga reptans *'Burgundy Glow'*
(pink-and-cream variegated
bugle)

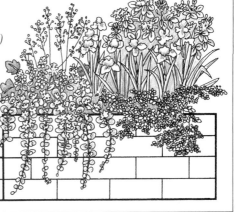

23

golden or blue needles, variegated ivies up the wall, and even a rose or two, you'll own a flower bed that never gets out of hand.

POTS, TUBS, TROUGHS AND SINKS

Growing plants in containers is exciting. For a start, you can grow *anything* in a pot, from an oak tree to a petunia, provided you realise that the larger trees will grow much more slowly than they would in open ground.

What's more, you can move your pots around to make different plant groups and effects. Tubs and sinks may be difficult to shift once planted, but even they can be shunted around every few years to change the scenery.

Any container will do, provided that it has ample drainage holes in the base. A container without holes will become waterlogged and the compost will turn sour – the holes are vital.

Having said that you can use anything, I do think that terracotta flower pots are the best. Make sure when you buy them that they are guaranteed frostproof. Some are not and begin to flake in the first winter.

Pots at least 10 inches (25 cm) in diameter are best. If they are smaller than this they dry out in the first rays of summer sunshine. But then, every container must be watered regularly, usually once a day, in summer – twice a day in really warm weather. Shortage of water is the commonest cause of failure – that and the wrong compost.

Garden soil is simply not good enough for plants in containers. It is badly drained in a confined space, and does not offer enough nutrients. Always use a proprietary potting compost.

The John Innes mixtures and peat-based composts are both suitable, but I find that my plants are happiest in a mixture of half-and-half John Innes No. 2 potting compost and a peat-based compost such as Levington or Arthur

Bowers. Shrubs such as rhododendrons, azaléas and camellias need lime-free compost. Try mixing John Innes ericaceous compost with a peat-based ericaceous compost. Both are lime-free.

It's always a good idea to put drainage material such as broken clay flower pot or gravel in the bottom of large flower pots to make sure the drainage hole stays unblocked.

Most shrubs and trees will need a larger pot and some extra compost every two years. Keep them happy in the interim with monthly feeds of dilute liquid fertiliser – liquid tomato fertiliser is best for any that are grown for flowers.

Troughs and sinks

Old stone troughs are something many gardeners would give their favourite spade for. They cost a fortune. Settle instead for making your own out of an old white porcelain butler's sink.

First, throw away the plug. Find help to carry the sink to your chosen spot, and raise it off the ground on a couple of concrete building blocks.

Clean it thoroughly and then coat the outside of the sink with a bonding agent such as 'Unibond' or 'Polybond'. Paint one side at a time and, when each is tacky, pat on your artificial stone mixture which can be made from 2 parts peat, 1 part sand and 1 part cement mixed to a stiff consistency with water. Apply the stone mixture ½ inch (1.25 cm) thick right down the sides and up and over the rim. Allow it to set for a couple of weeks before putting gravel or broken flower pots in the base and then filling up with potting compost.

Many gardeners grow alpines and rock-plants in sinks. These little beauties enjoy really well-drained compost so add some sharp sand or grit to John Innes No. 1 potting compost.

Fill to within a couple of inches (5

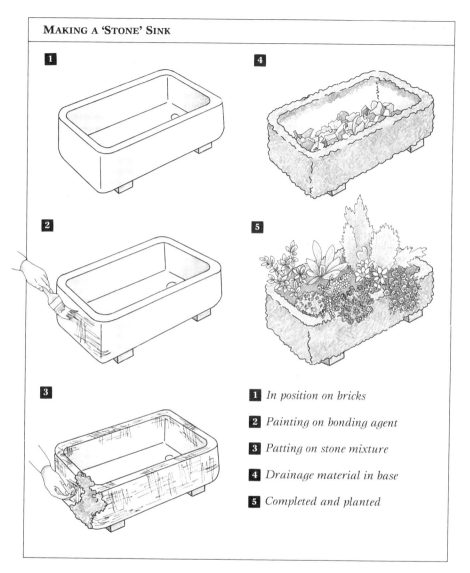

1 *In position on bricks*

2 *Painting on bonding agent*

3 *Patting on stone mixture*

4 *Drainage material in base*

5 *Completed and planted*

cm) of the rim and then plant your alpines. Add a dwarf conifer such as the Noah's ark juniper (*Juniperus communis* 'Compressa'), and make sure you use rock-plants that are not too rampant.

Cover the surface of the compost with about an inch (2.5 cm) of sharp gravel to show the plants off well and prevent them from being splashed with mud. Hey presto! One instant alpine garden.

Rock-plants for sink gardens

Androsace (rock jasmine), armeria (thrift), dianthus (alpine pinks), gen-

25

tians, edelweiss, lewisia, saxifrages, sempervivums (houseleeks), thymes.

WINDOW-BOXES AND HANGING BASKETS

Within the backyard, or even if you've no backyard at all, window-boxes on your outside sills and hanging baskets slung from the walls will provide colour at or near eye level.

Window-boxes need to be stout. The compost they contain weighs quite a lot when it's moist, and a flimsy box will fall apart when you try to lift it.

Buy your box (in which case it will probably be made of rigid plastic) or make it out of timber. Either way, there should be drainage holes in the base, and a couple of feet to hold the base of the box clear of the sill.

Alternatively, support the box in front of the windowsill on really sturdy angle brackets. Plug the wall and then screw the brackets into position, leaning on them to make sure they are capable of sustaining the weight of the full and planted box.

Paint, varnish or timber preservative will be necessary if the box is made of wood.

Put the box in position before filling it with compost. Use the same mixture recommended for pots (see previous page) and don't forget a layer of drainage material in the base.

Window-boxes can be purely seasonal, in which case they are planted up in autumn with spring-flowering bulbs such as dwarf narcissi, dwarf irises, dwarf tulips, crocuses and scillas, along with 'Universal' pansies and polyanthus. When these fade in late spring they are pulled out and replaced with summer bedding plants such as petunias, ageratum, pelargoniums (geraniums), ivy-leafed geraniums, lobelia, verbena, French marigolds, begonias, dwarf asters and trailing fuchsias. Avoid tall plants which will rob your rooms of light.

On the other hand, the box can have a few permanent residents: a central dwarf conifer, variegated ivies trailing down the front, a couple of winter-flowering heathers – one at each end – and spring and summer bloomers can be planted in between them and removed when they fade.

Change some of the compost once a year when you change over the plants and they'll maintain their vigour.

Water well in dry weather, and feed once a week from May to September with dilute liquid tomato fertiliser – your window-boxes will bloom brilliantly.

Whichever system you choose, you'll wonder why you didn't do it years ago.

Hanging baskets

Hanging baskets really are best used only in summer, unless you want to risk planting up 'Universal' pansies in winter and hope that the weather is kind.

Baskets made of wire make it possible to plant them up not only on top but down the sides as well. Those made of rigid plastic, while being easier to plant up and having a drip tray to keep your head dry, are less spectacular when fully furnished.

Plant up hanging baskets in the comfort of a greenhouse or porch during mid- to late April. Line the basket with a proprietary liner or with green sphagnum moss which can be bought from a florist.

Stand the basket on a large flower pot or a bucket to plant it up. Line with a little moss in the base, add a little compost (peat-based potting compost is lightest) and insert your plants, roots first, around the base. Add more lining material if necessary, then more compost and more plants until eventually the sides are fully planted. Allow 4 to 6 inches (10-15 cm) between plants. Plant up the top last and then suspend the basket before watering it well.

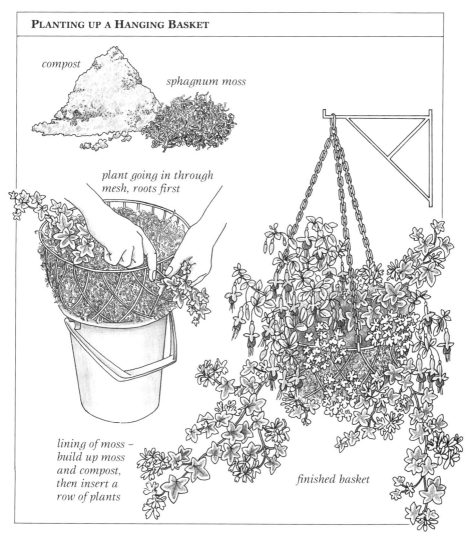

compost

sphagnum moss

plant going in through
mesh, roots first

lining of moss –
build up moss
and compost,
then insert a
row of plants

finished basket

As far as plants are concerned, trailers are best, with just one or two bushy plants in the top of the basket. Try ivy-leafed geraniums, yellow-leafed creeping jenny (*Lysimachia nummularia* 'Aurea'), trailing lobelia, *Helichrysum petiolatum*, pendulous begonias, and trailing fuchsias and verbena.

Baskets can be hung outside in late May or early June and left until the frosts of autumn polish them off. Do make sure that the brackets used to hold them are fastened securely to the wall.

The secret of success is regular watering. Water them daily – twice daily when it's sunny – and feed them once a week with dilute liquid tomato fertiliser. Dry baskets are dead baskets. Moist ones are monstrous pleasures.

27

ROSES

A garden without roses is like gravy without meat. Wonderful bushes they are. All right, so they need pruning and the occasional spray to bump off greenfly, but if you choose the right varieties you can enjoy flowers from early summer to autumn, without having to brandish the secateurs and the sprayer too often .

There are many types of rose. These are the main ones –

Hybrid teas or large-flowered roses

These are the fat and pointed roses that win prizes as single blooms in flower shows. Each stem carries only a few flowers and the blooms come in flushes.

Floribunda or cluster-flowered roses

Better for massing in rose beds. More flowers are produced on each stem and flowering is more or less continuous throughout the summer. Hybrid teas and floribundas are collectively known as 'bush roses'.

Standard roses

Hybrid teas or floribundas grown on a tall stem.

Miniature roses

Small roses between 6 and 18 inches (15–45 cm) high. Quite hardy and far better grown in the garden than as house plants (which is what they are sometimes sold as).

Climbing and rambling roses

Although they don't strictly climb, these roses send out long stems that can be tied in to walls and fences. The repeat-flowering ('recurrent') kinds are best; others have just one glorious season of bloom in early summer.

Shrub roses

Often larger than 'bush roses', the shrubs include the 'old-fashioned roses' that are so popular today. Many of them date back to the nineteenth and even to the eighteenth century, they have exquisite fragrances and, often, fairly disease-resistant foliage. Although some have just one flush of flower in early summer, many of them are repeat-flowering and some carry ornamental hips.

PLANTING

Roses are sold 'bare-root' between November and March. This means they've been dug up from the nursery, cut back and packaged with no soil clinging to the roots. They'll transplant with very little shock to their system.

They are also sold growing in containers, in which case they can be planted at any time of year, even when in flower. Your new rose should have at least three stems.

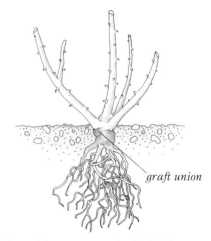

graft union

Planted bare-root rose bush, showing level of graft union below soil level

28

Roses are greedy. They'll grow on most soils but they do like plenty of oomph at their roots. Dig in oodles of garden compost or well-rotted manure, and make sure the bed or border is in full sun. Plant them so that the graft union (where the stems of the rose join the rootstock or briar on to which they are grafted) is buried just below the surface of the soil. A good dusting of blood, bone and fishmeal will help them to take off.

As far as spacing goes, that depends very much on variety. Hybrid teas and floribundas can be planted 2 feet (60 cm) apart; shrub roses need rather more.

Climbers and ramblers planted next to walls and fences should have plenty of organic matter at their roots to hold on to moisture in what is usually a very dry spot.

Tie their stems in to horizontal wires fastened to masonry nails at 18-inch (45-cm) intervals up the wall.

During their first season, keep an eye on them for water and don't allow them to be thirsty.

PRUNING

Judging by my postbag, this is one of the biggest problems ever faced. The stems never seem to be evenly spaced and the buds aren't where you want them. What's more, the technique is different for each kind of rose.

Not to worry; here's my 'at-a-glance' guide to pruning the different kinds of roses. All you need is a sharp pair of secateurs and, for older bushes, a pair of loppers or a pruning saw. And just remember that roses haven't read books, so they're not even aware that they need to be pruned.

Hybrid teas
New bushes should be pruned after planting. February is a good time. Cut them right down to 3 or 4 inches (8–10 cm), making your cuts above outward-

facing buds (if you can see them). In future years prune between January and March. Cut out dead wood. Cut out weak or diseased wood. Cut out stems that cross the centre of the bush. On old bushes, cut out some gnarled stems each year. When you've done that, shorten all the remaining stems to about 1 foot (30 cm) – again cutting just above an outward-facing bud.

Floribundas
As for hybrid teas but not quite so low. Cut back newly planted bushes to 6 inches (15 cm), mature bushes to 18 inches (45 cm).

Standard roses
Treat the bush on top of the single stem like a hybrid tea or floribunda.

Miniatures
Simply snip out dead and overcrowding shoots in March.

Shrub roses
Prune them in February or March, snipping out dead stems and dead shoot tips. Other than this all you need to do is snip out one or two old stems if the bush becomes really overcrowded.

Climbing roses
Cut off dead shoot tips in March and cut back side-shoots to 4 inches (10 cm). One or two very old stems can be removed if the plant has plenty of young ones.

Rambling roses
Prune immediately after flowering, removing one or two old stems (as with climbers) and shortening side-shoots to 4 inches (10 cm). If no new shoots are produced, retain the old ones as long as they flower well.

Feeding
Give your roses two helpings of rose fertiliser every year – once in March

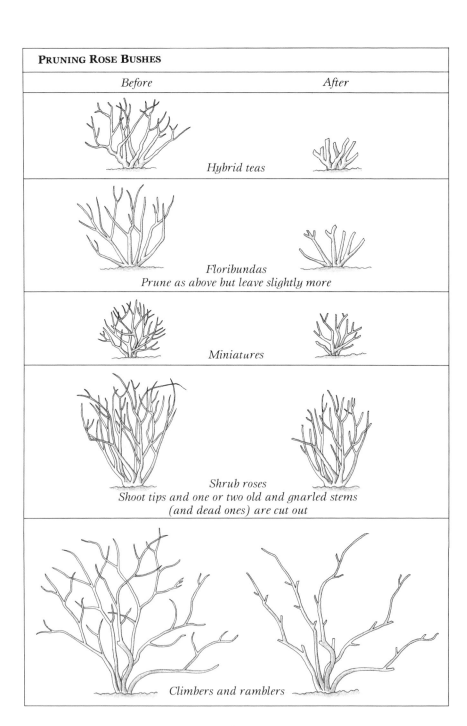

PRUNING ROSE BUSHES

Before	After

Hybrid teas

Floribundas
Prune as above but leave slightly more

Miniatures

Shrub roses
Shoot tips and one or two old and gnarled stems
(and dead ones) are cut out

Climbers and ramblers

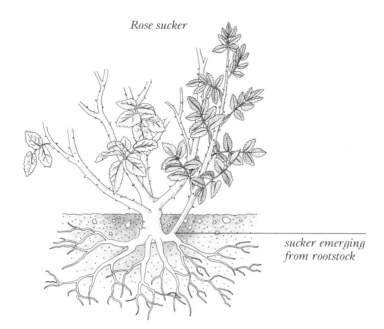

Rose sucker

*sucker emerging
from rootstock*

and again in June. Sprinkle it on the soil around the bushes and hoe it in.

Mulching
Spreading manure around the bushes in spring helps to retain moisture and improve the food supply. It keeps down weeds, too.

Dead-heading
Snip off faded flowers as soon as they have gone over, unless the variety produces ornamental hips.

Suckers
Suckers are shoots that come from the rootstock or briar. You'll recognise them by their different leaves. Scrape away the soil and pull them off where they emerge from the root.

Pests and diseases
Greenfly, mildew and blackspot are the main rose diseases. They can all be kept under control by spraying at the first sign of attack with one of the 'cocktail' sprays especially developed for roses such as 'Roseclear' or 'Multirose'.

Gather up and burn all fallen leaves at the end of the season to prevent blackspot recurring year after year. Better still, grow roses with thick leaves that are resistant to the disease.

Varieties
When it comes to choosing varieties, rely on the catalogues of specialist rose nurseries. They'll tell you which varieties have the best scent and the best disease-resisting qualities. They will also indicate size and spread so you can make sure the bushes will fit into your garden.

If you want to know where to find a particular variety, invest in a copy of *Find That Rose*, which can be obtained by post from The Rose Growers Association, 303 Mile End Road, Colchester CO4 5EA, price £1 including postage.

31

Everyone has their own favourites when it comes to roses, and these are some of mine. The main attributes of any rose, I reckon, should be beauty, fragrance and disease resistance. Most of these possess all three, but sometimes they're allowed to get away with two!

Hybrid teas

'Alec's Red' – rich crimson with a strong fragrance

'Alexander' – vermilion, slight fragrance

'Ena Harkness' – deep, rich crimson (even though she hangs her head a little she's a cracker!)

'Fragrant Cloud' – rosy red and very fragrant

'Grandpa Dickson' – pale yellow, huge flowers

'Just Joey' – apricot orange

'Mischief' – coral pink, slight fragrance

'Pascali' – the best white

'Peace' – large pale yellow blooms, edged pink

'Silver Jubilee' – a confection of pinks; good fragrance

'Wendy Cussons' cerise pink, strong fragrance

'Whisky Mac' – rich coppery orange

Floribundas

'Allgold' – bright yellow, slight fragrance

'Arthur Bell' – yellow, fading to cream; strong fragrance

'City of Belfast' – bright scarlet

'English Miss' – soft pink, strong fragrance

'Eye Paint' – masses of small red single flowers with white eyes

'Iceberg' – white, slight fragrance

'Korresia' – bright yellow, slight fragrance

'Margaret Merrill' – white with a stunning fragrance

'Pink Parfait' – pink with creamy highlights

'Queen Elizabeth' – tall and vigorous pink

'Southampton' – apricot orange

'Sue Lawley' – rich pink edged white, semi-double

'Trumpeter' – bright red

'Yesterday' – lilac pink and white, semi-double

Shrub roses

'Alchemist – 10 ft × 8 ft (300 cm × 240 cm), yellow flushed apricot

'Ballerina' – 4 ft × 4 ft (120 cm × 120 cm), hundreds of small pink and white flowers

'Buff Beauty' – 6 ft × 6 ft (180 cm × 180 cm), buff orange, semi-double

'Canary Bird' – 6 ft × 6 ft (180 cm × 180 cm), bright yellow single flowers

'Cardinal de Richelieu' – 4 ft × 3 ft (120 cm × 90 cm), dusky purple

'Chapeau de Napoleon' – 5 ft × 4 ft (150 cm × 120 cm), pink with mossy buds

'Complicata' – 8 ft × 8 ft (240 cm × 240 cm), single pink and white flowers

'Cornelia' – 5 ft × 6 ft (150 cm × 180 cm), apricot pink

'Fantin-Latour' – 6 ft × 5 ft (180 cm × 150 cm), pale pink, flattened double

'Frau Dagmar Hartopp' – 4 ft × 5 ft (120 cm × 150 cm), single pink flowers; fat red hips to follow

'Frühlingsgold' – 8 ft × 6 ft (240 cm × 180 cm), bright primrose yellow, semi-double

'Frühlingsmorgen – 6 ft × 5 ft (180 cm × 150 cm), rich pink with primrose-yellow eye

'Golden Wings' – 5 ft × 5 ft (150 cm × 150 cm), pale gold

'Königin von Dänemark' – 5 ft × 4 ft (150 cm ×120 cm), double pink flowers

'Lady Penzance' – 6 ft × 6 ft (180 cm × 180 cm), single bright rose pink flowers, good hips

'Madame Hardy' – 5 ft × 5 ft (150 cm × 150 cm), pure white fully double blooms

'Madame Pierre Oger' – 4 ft × 4 ft (120 cm × 120 cm), shell pink

'Maiden's Blush' – 5 ft × 5 ft (150 cm × 150 cm), blush pink

'Marguerite Hilling' – 7 ft × 7 ft (210 cm × 210 cm), warm pink, semi-double flowers

'Nevada' – 7 ft × 7 ft (210 cm × 210 cm), creamy white, semi-double

'Reine des Violettes' – 6 ft × 6 ft (180 cm × 180 cm), violet-purple

Rosa gallica 'Versicolor' ('Rosa Mundi') – 5 ft × 5 ft (150 cm × 150 cm), masses of pink and white candy-striped flowers

Rosa moyesii 'Geranium' – 8 ft × 8 ft (240 cm × 240 cm), single rich red flowers followed by long scarlet hips

Rosa rubrifolia – 7 ft × 7 ft (210 cm × 210 cm), blue-grey leaves (red when young) and single pink flowers followed by dark red hips

'Roseraie de l'Hay' – 6 ft × 5 ft (180 cm × 150 cm), rough green leaves and double magenta flowers

'Stanwell Perpetual' – 5 ft × 5 ft (150 cm × 150 cm), blush pink

Miniatures

'Angela Rippon' – salmon pink

'Baby Faurax' – purplish pink

'Darling Flame' – orange and yellow

'Josephine Wheatcroft' – yellow

'Magic Carrousel' – white, deeply flushed pink at the edges

'New Penny' – rich pink

'Snow Carpet' – white

Climbers

'Aloha' – rich pink, fully double

'Bantry Bay' – soft pink

'Compassion' – pink flushed apricot

'Crimson Glory' (climbing) – rich crimson

'Iceberg' (climbing) – white

'Gloire de Dijon' – buff to pale orange

'Golden Showers' – clear yellow

'Handel' – white, edged pink, fully double

'Mermaid' – single yellow, amber stamens

'Pink Perpetué' – rose pink

'Schoolgirl' – apricot

'Zéphirine Drouhin' – cerise pink, thornless

Ramblers

'Albéric Barbier' – creamy yellow

'Albertine' – pink tinged with salmon

'American Pillar' – deep pink with white eye; rich green foliage

'Félicité et Perpétué' – creamy white

'Kiftsgate' – monster with hundreds of small white flowers; only for training over large sheds or apple trees

'New Dawn' – pale pink

'Veilchenblau' – masses of small pale violet flowers; good fragrance

BULBS

You can have disasters with any kind of plant, but bulbs are more foolproof than most. Each one is like a firework, only instead of lighting the blue touch paper, all you have to do is add water and stand well back.

Most gardeners think of bulbs as spring flowers – daffodils, tulips and the like. But there are also bulbs like lilies which are brilliant in summer. All can be relied on to bloom again year after year if you treat them in the right way.

BULBS IN THE GARDEN

Bulbs that are to be planted in the garden need to be treated considerately. They'll always do their best, but their best is better if you're good to them. Plant them in open and sunny spots. Snowdrops will do reasonably well in shade, as will tuberous-rooted wood anemones, but the vast majority like good light. They also enjoy good soil, not the poor and rooty stuff they are likely to find right under trees. Waterlogged soil will almost always cause them to rot off, so make sure the earth is well drained.

Planting depth varies from bulb to bulb, but, as a rule of thumb, each bulb needs to be planted in a hole that is three times its own depth. That means a daffodil bulb measuring 2 inches (5 cm) from top to toe should be planted in a hole 6 inches (15 cm) deep. It seems a lot, but plant any shallower and your bulbs will go short of food and water in dry summers.

In beds and borders, bulbs can be planted in groups, or spaced more evenly right along the bed. Avoid spacing them too far apart, though, or placing them in serried ranks; your display will look either mean or military.

Daffodils, narcissi, snowdrops and crocuses can all be 'naturalised' in grass. Plant them with a trowel or special bulb planter in unevenly shaped drifts. Small bulbs or corms, such as crocuses, can be planted under a lifted square of turf – it makes the job quicker.

Use your common sense when it comes to spacing. Small bulbs or corms like crocuses can be 2 inches (5 cm) apart; daffodil bulbs should be about 4 inches (10 cm) apart.

Plant spring-flowering bulbs in September or October. No harm will come to them if you plant them right up to Christmas, but after that you run the risk of them flowering very late.

After the flowers fade, allow the foliage to flop for six weeks before it is cut off. Don't be tempted to tie it up with elastic bands – it won't be able to feed properly. It's worth remembering this drawback when you plant bulbs in the garden. Plant them where their foliage won't be too much of a nuisance.

Scatter blood, bone and fishmeal around the bulbs when they are in flower. That means they'll be well nourished while they are producing next year's flowers.

Snowdrops are best planted 'in the green', which means while they are in leaf. There's a higher survival rate than when they are planted dry. Beg some from a friend in February or March, or order from a specialist supplier.

Not all bulbs planted in the garden are best left undisturbed. Gladioli (planted in March or April for summer flowers) should be dug up and dried off in October and stored in a frost-free shed or garage during the winter.

Lilies can be planted in early spring among other border plants, but put sand in the bottom of each hole to make sure the drainage is good, and mark their site with a cane so you don't hoe them up.

Crown imperials (*Fritillaria imperialis*) are best planted on their sides. Don't ask me why; it just seems to make them flower better.

Be handy with the slug pellets with lilies and crown imperials – molluscs love 'em when they're pushing through the soil.

Dahlias

Although not strictly bulbs, dahlias grow from fat tubers that are equally effective storage organs. These tubers can be bought from shops, nurseries and garden centres in spring, pre-packed in bags equipped with glossy colour photographs.

There are many different flower types, from the small and dainty pompoms, to the larger, decorative and spiky cactus-flowered types, ranging in colour from white through yellow, orange, red, purple and lilac (but there's no blue!).

Dahlias are meaty plants requiring rich soil to do well. Beef it up with well-rotted garden compost or manure, at around two bucketfuls to the square yard (sq m), and plant the tubers 4 to 6 inches (10-15 cm) deep soil 2 to 3 feet (60-90 cm) apart depending on the ultimate size of the plants. Plant in early May and then scatter blood, bone and fish meal over the soil – two handfuls to the square yard (sq m) – and hoe it in. As soon as shoots emerge, knock in a stout dahlia stake alongside each tuber so that the fleshy stems can be tied in as they grow. Smaller-flowered and shorter-growing varieties may be self-supporting, but the larger-flowered types will topple unless fastened to something that can take their weight.

Depth	Daffodils/ narcissi	Tulips	Crocuses	Snow- drops	Dwarf irises	Hardy cyclamen	Lilies	Crown imperials	Gladioli	Colchicums
BULB PLANTING CHART										
1 in (2.5 cm)										
2 in (5 cm)										
3 in (7.5 cm)										
4 in (10 cm)										
5 in (12.5 cm)										
6 in (15 cm)										
7 in (17.5 cm)										
8 in (20 cm)										
9 in (23 cm)										

When the flower buds form, pinch out the two on either side of the central one to produce a decent sized bloom that could do well for itself at your local flower show.

Water the plants well in dry spells, and feed them once a fortnight with dilute liquid tomato fertiliser.

Cut the blooms regularly to keep them coming, and trap earwigs (those pincer-tailed pests that love nibbling dahlia flowers) in flower pots that are stuffed with newspaper and up-ended on bamboo canes among the plants. The earwigs love the shelter these upside-down pots provide and run inside to keep warm. Knock them out into a bucket of water whenever you're passing.

In autumn, when frost blackens the leaves and stems, cut off the top growth, leaving just 4 inches (10 cm) of stem at the bottom and dig up the tubers. Dry them off in an airy shed or garage, and then store them there in boxes of dry peat until they can be planted in the garden again.

BULBS IN POTS

Christmas just wouldn't be Christmas without a few potted bulbs – their scent is as tantalising as that of turkey.

Narcissi such as 'Grande Soleil d'Or' and 'Paper White' are all headily fragrant and easy to find in nurseries and garden centres in September and October.

Plant up one pot every two weeks so that you've half a dozen pots to hand. Choose 6-inch (15-cm) or 8-inch (20-cm) pots and use peat-based potting compost. Bulb fibre is quite unnecessary. It was originally made for bowls without holes (to keep the compost sweet). I reckon all bowls and pots should have holes to get rid of excess water, which is why I stick to ordinary potting compost.

Put some compost in the bottom of the pot, then a layer of bulbs, then

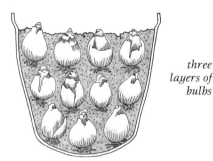

three layers of bulbs

Daffodils in a pot

more compost, then more bulbs, finishing off with a layer of compost so that the noses of the top layer of bulbs are showing through.

Water the pot and stand it in a cool, dark place for six weeks (a shed, garage or cellar). Then bring it into the light and gradually introduce it to higher temperatures (start it off in an unheated bedroom and 10 days later move it to the sitting room). Twiggy pea-sticks or split green canes encircled by green twine will give support to flopping flowers.

Hyacinths are best planted in shallow bowls in a single layer. Their noses should be visible after planting, and their treatment is the same as for the narcissi.

After flowering, pot-grown bulbs are best thrown away. I know that will make me unpopular, but I've had enough of spearing unidentified bulbous objects on the end of my garden fork to last me a lifetime.

Crocuses can often be quite tricky to grow in pots, often producing a forest of foliage and very few flowers.

The secret is to keep them cool for the regulation eight weeks after potting, and then still keep them cool when they are brought into the house. That way the flowers will be pushed up clear of the foliage, rather than the rushy leaves towering above the blooms.

Take care not to overwater crocuses. That's another state of affairs that can encourage leaf growth at the expense of the flowers. The compost should be kept evenly moist at all times, not wringing wet, and crocus corms, like bulbs, should be planted in containers equipped with drainage holes. Discard them after flowering, unless you adore filling corners of your garden with unidentified bulbous objects.

Lilies in pots

Often far easier than they are in the garden, three lily bulbs can be planted in a 10-inch (25-cm) pot of John Innes No. 2 potting compost with a little sharp sand added. The bulbs should be just covered, and plenty of drainage material should be put in the base before the compost goes in.

Plant your bulbs in early spring and stand them outdoors against the house wall for shelter. As the shoots emerge, sprinkle a few slug pellets on the soil. During the summer, feed the pot with dilute liquid tomato fertiliser every couple of weeks, and when the stems die down at the end of summer, chop them off just above the compost and stand the pots by the house wall once more.

The bulbs will grow happily like this for a good three years, flowering well every summer, and you can choose varieties of lily that flower at any time between June and September. If I had to limit myself to just two liles, they would be *Lilium regale* - 4-5 feet (120-150 cm), with white trumpets in June or July flushed mauve on the outside and deliciously scented, and *Lilium speciosum rubrum*, which is the same height but carries its Turk's cap type flowers in late summer. They are white, heavily suffused with rosy red.

Hippeastrums

Often known as amaryllis, the hippeastrum is that massive bulb that produces a stout stalk, atop which flowers reminiscent of agricultural show loudspeakers are carried. They can be red, pink or white.

Plant the bulb in autumn, choosing a pot that is only slightly larger in diameter than the bulb. Use John Innes No. 2 potting compost and make it moist at planting time so that very little water need be given while the flower stalk is expanding. Pot up the bulb so that only the lower half is covered with compost.

Stand it indoors on a sunny windowsill, and be very sparing with the water until the flowers have faded. That's when leaves start to appear. Give the plant dilute liquid tomato food once a week when the leaves are expanding, until August when all further water and food is withheld. Let the compost dry out and in October chop off the leaves a couple of inches (5 cm) above the bulb.

Now here is the secret of success! To get your bulb to flower again, knock it out of its pot, remove the compost and stand it in the airing cupboard for three weeks to encourage flower bud initiation. Store the bulb in a cool and dark place after this until you're ready to plant again.

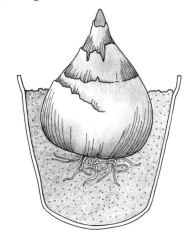

Hippeastrum bulb potted

CELEBRITY GARDENS

THORA HIRD AND MINE

I don't know about you, but I'm incorrigibly nosy. Give me a chance to poke around a stately home and I'm fascinated to see how the other half lives. But I'm also interested to see how they garden, and courtesy of *Daytime Live* I managed to wangle a guided tour of several celebrity gardens. While they may not be stately, they certainly reflect the preferences and passions of the folk that live there.

Where to start, that was the problem. I rang Thora Hird, who's a great lady and no mean gardener.

'How about letting me look round your garden?' I asked. 'I'd rather look round yours,' she said. So that's how we started.

We've lived in our house in Hampshire for about eight years now. When we came here the one-in-four hillside was just a rough orchard with a corrugated iron shed half-way up that the estate agent grandly called a stable block. It was anything but stable. One great heave and it fell over, but its timbers did make a warming bonfire.

Over the years the half-acre of garden with an acre of paddock at the top has been turned into my kind of garden. I'd always wanted a big garden, having had three – during my childhood, adolescence and early married life – that were no more than 20 feet long or wide.

There are bits of formality, and bits of billowing country naturalness. Thora seemed to like what she saw and related her own stories of gardening as a child.

There were the seeds of Virginian stock she sowed in garden soil dumped in an orange box. On top of them she piled horse manure: 'Only one seed grew, but you should have seen it; it was three feet tall if it was an inch!'

Now she and her husband share a Sussex garden with her daughter Jeanette Scott and family. In it grows the golden feverfew I gave Thora a couple of years ago. I only gave her one plant. She now has hundreds. Mind you, I can't understand why she turned down the offer of a bit of variegated ground elder. It's a wonderful ground cover plant and so pretty. Ah well, I suppose Thora knows best.

I did worry whether or not she'd make it up the slope, but she did, and enjoyed the view, too.

I'm a great looker in the garden. No; I'm not referring to my handsome physique, just the fact that I like lots of places to stop and stare.

There are patches to suit all moods: old-fashioned roses with their exquisite scents, and bits of woodland garden under trees. One patch of grass erupts with daffodils and narcissi in spring, and border perennials are mixed with annual bedding plants for summer colour.

There's a backbone of evergreens (not too many or the garden would look like a cemetery), and a few trees to give height and scale. You know, when you're making a large garden from scratch, it takes that much longer for trees and shrubs to assume their proper scale. That's why the white bridge that crosses a pebble river bed and a small pool looks so dominant at the moment. But when the nearby birch trees have grown they'll make the bridge seem smaller.

I love secret corners, so there are winding paths that tempt you to explore, and there's a vegetable patch, too, with water provided courtesy of a large oak water butt fitted with a cast iron 'village pump'.

Garden ornaments are essential, but I can't stand gnomes or concrete damsels. That's why I use white beehives, old iron gatepost finials, large terracotta flowerpots and rhubarb forcers instead. They complement the plants rather than insult them.

The soil is lousy – chalk, clay and flint – but with lashings of garden compost and hefty helpings of manure from the local stables, I feel I'm winning.

I don't spray much. Only the occasional bash to get rid of greenfly on the roses, but I do try to be kind to my plants and feed them with good old blood, bone and fishmeal every spring.

As a result, I've so far counted 43 species of bird in my garden, plus slow-worms, hedgehogs, rabbits, foxes and deer. Oh, and Thora Hird as well.

I've also been lucky in finding good helpers. I don't have a full-time gardener, but the two part-timers I've had over the last few years have done everything I should be doing when I'm away showing other people what to do with their gardens. To Sue and Doug I owe great thanks.

ANITA RODDICK

It takes imagination, foresight, skill, good business sense, a smattering of luck and a giant-sized helping of tenacity for anyone to succeed in commerce. If she's a woman the chances are that these qualities need to be multiplied by 10. Anita Roddick multiplied them by 100 and came up with Body Shop, which started as one small emporium and now has branches all over Britain and in other corners of the world too.

A recent newspaper survey placed her among the 200 richest people in Britain. She sounded a terrifying prospect, but a woman who's so keen on gardening must have a soft centre. So steadying my nerve, I set off for her house in Sussex.

Once the property of Arthur Rackham, the large and rambling house was surrounded by a dismal plot of land when the Roddicks took it on, with no sign of those wizened and gnarled tree trunks that appeared so often in his illustrations.

That was five years ago. Bulldozers moved in and made a garden according to the Roddick requirements, along with a helpful landscape architect.

I asked if she found gardening relaxing. 'Tremendously. This is my alternative to Librium and Valium. Just to come out here gives me a chance to switch off.'

And switch off she does, among beds and borders so lush and established that I found it hard to believe they were only four years old. What was the secret of their growth?

'An underground irrigation system. It pops up every day when the soil looks a bit dry, and when it's given it a soak it pops down again.'

Judging by the puddles on the path the sunny morning we walked around, I guess it had been on that morning. They didn't make walking difficult, but they did make for a rather damp game of draughts. Not the normal board game, you understand, but a huge garden draught-board made of pink and white concrete slabs, fitted with 'draughtsmen' fully 2 feet (60 cm) across and fashioned out of fibreglass. She won, but then she usually does.

Wit and humour feature frequently in the Roddicks' garden. Children are encouraged to enjoy it as much as adults. That's why there's a huge rainbow with a crock of large gold coins at the end of it – the coins can be hidden for a treasure hunt. The pool is fitted with a waterfall up which plastic goldfish appear to be leaping, and a statue is playing a solo game of boule down a long grass avenue.

Much of the planting is muted – greens, yellows and whites – but there are moments when Anita's Italian extraction breaks out into floods of colour. She loves geraniums, but hates 'piddling patches of daffodils around trees in grass'.

There are places to sit, and viewpoints that offer panoramas of the Sussex downs, but there's also a dark alleyway down the side of the kitchen where everything refused to grow. It's been turned into a narrow Japanese garden. Gravel covers the soil, bamboo fences have been erected, and Japanese maples nestle alongside a stone temple. Living bamboos can cope with the shade that the favourite scarlet geraniums found impossible to enjoy.

This is a garden that has not been made on a shoestring. The formal pools, the pink gazebo and other appointments smack of high finance, but the things Anita Roddick cherishes most are the moments of pleasure that the garden can give in return. Like the night the children had their friends around for a party. Anita Roddick strolled out to find them swirling round the lawn to Bruce Springsteen's 'Dancing in the Dark' – 'I'll never forget that; it was pure magic.'

SIR HARDY AMIES

The garden of a court couturier was something I itched to see. Would it be high fashion? Would it have a regal bearing? Sir Hardy Amies, after all, has designed dresses for the Queen for the last 40 years.

The garden fulfilled both requirements completely. It is laid out behind an old Oxfordshire schoolhouse in what was once the playground (fortunately not tarmacked). High walls surround it and it is completely formal.

Sir Hardy (wearing dark green trousers of fine tweed and a cable-stitched pullover of a complementary shade) reclined in a garden chair and expounded his ideas of gardening.

'A garden behind a small house simply must be formal.'

'Couldn't that lead to boredom?' I asked.

'Do you think my garden is boring?'

'Er, no.'

'It must reflect the lines of the house, and these informal and sweeping curves one so often sees simply do not do that.'

I joined him on a stroll round the garden which is barely more than 50 feet square, but feels much larger.

'The paths are all large enough for two people to walk side by side; that's very important.'

One large central path was obviously the main axis of the garden (I was catching on quickly) and was a good 6 feet (1.8 m) wide.

'It used, in the olden days, to be called a forthright, and I think that's rather a good term for it, don't you?'

I did. The forthright led to a handsome stone gazebo, inside which was erected a huge slate tablet with a Latin inscription indicating (Sir Hardy explained) who had made the garden and when.

Flanking the forthright were two rectangular beds of soil edged with close-clipped box and filled with shrub roses. Sir Hardy is a shrub-rose addict. Their French names trip off his tongue with ease: 'Yvonne Rabier' and 'Souvenir du Dr Jamain'. In summer they are underplanted with tobacco plants.

The walls surrounding the garden support climbing roses like 'Sombreuil' and 'New Dawn' which are mingled with clematis, and below them are raised beds filled with silver-foliage plants and headily scented pinks. There's also room for herbs and rockplants; encrusted saxifrages grow out of niches in the warm grey walls, and rows of lavender bushes sit below them.

The whole thing is, as you would expect, beautifully tailored and tastefully colour schemed, with no strident oranges and vermilions, and no tasteless pieces of cheap statuary. The two stone pyramids that stand sentinel in front of the gazebo were made locally after their two canework predecessors fell to bits. Sir Hardy is not at all averse to having things tailor-made himself.

I did spot just one touch of vanity. In the centre of the cobbled forthright were picked out the initials HA.

'Yes. I'm not sure about that. If you really want to know, I think it's rather naff.'

Not, I think, a description that would apply to the rest of Sir Hardy Amies's designer garden.

JILLY COOPER

She's a wordsmith *par excellence* who crafted the bonniest *mots* in her *Sunday Times* column for several years, and then went on to establish herself as a best-seller writer. I've curled up with her *Riders* which accompanied me on a Mediterranean cruise, and I've read *Rivals*, about the back-stabbing world of television, thinking that perhaps I mix with the wrong people.

Jilly Cooper doesn't so much bubble as fizz, in an Angela Brazil sort of way. The resulting nickname of 'Jolly Sooper' is one she must take in good part, since she used it as a title for a trio of books containing her *Sunday Times* nuggets. But beneath the often saucy image is a sensitive and astonishingly hard-working woman.

Walk round her garden when the weather is anything like reasonable and you'll hear, among the 'chook-chook-chook' of the blackbirds and the distant mooing of cows, the clack-clack-clack of the typewriter. Mrs Cooper's next manuscript is being belted out on a portable typewriter set on a table underneath the honeyed walls of the Cotswold house.

It seems as though she's hardly off the TV screens – acting as a panellist on *What's My Line?* or appearing on a chat show – but the truth is that during the writing of one of her blockbusters (and for me they bust blocks far more engagingly than those of heavier-handed lady writers) she's emphatic that she does not leave home for any reason.

So it is that the garden has become an office as well as a place for pleasure. Jilly's husband Leo Cooper is a publisher of military books who admits that he's never read any of his wife's offerings. But then she's probably not read *Jane's Fighting Ships* either.

Their garden is a team effort with a degree of Sissinghurst about it – not so much in the apparent similarity to that Kent garden, but in that Leo Cooper acts as the grand architect (rather like Harold Nicolson) and Jilly has a bit of Vita Sackville-West about her. But only a bit.

Once the chantry where monks sang and were buried, the Cooper house is a vast and rambling stone pile of the sort that cries out for roses round the door and honeysuckle over an archway, and it gets them.

Jilly loves rustic poles, and had them put in a row alongside one of the lawns. Leo can't abide them and had them taken out.

'We argue about the garden a lot. He hates poles and I love them. I can't stand brilliant flowers like French marigolds so I won't have them.'

She has her theories about colour scheming. 'Fair women like me always go for soft, pastel colours like pink and pale blue. Dark women like stronger colours – that's why you see so many reds and oranges in Spain and Italy,'

The beds and borders around the house reflect this. They are crammed to overflowing with shrub roses and border plants – catmint, valerian, delphiniums and buttercups all rolled into one huge floral carpet. I visited it in June and was told that this was its best time of year. The vegetable patch was a sea of buttercups and bindweed ('we had to let it go') and tidiness was not the garden's strongest point. For me that was a bonus. I like to see gardens that are loved but not nagged to death.

'Its peak really only lasts about three weeks,' said Jilly, 'and I'm afraid there's not much to see in late summer.'

I looked across the garden towards the distant Cotswold hills. In the field of cows below the ha-ha, a white calf frolicked among the buttercups.

'He's called "Lovely Spot",' said Jilly.

'Why's that?' I asked.

'Because people always come out here and look across the field and say "What a lovely spot!"'

And it is. Or rather, they both are.

VIEWERS' PROBLEMS

Gardeners' lives are beset with difficulties, and I have a postbag that makes many of Claire Rayner's problems seem comparatively simple. It's so easy to become a worrier, and there are worries that crop up time and time again. Here's my list of the commonest, along with their solutions. I'm not saying they're all easy to solve, but they can sometimes be made less mountainous.

Ground elder

This is the biggest problem weed in every English garden, or so it seems. The leaves do look a bit like elder, and the white flowers are like a coarse cow parsley. The thick white roots get everywhere and choke out border plants and small shrubs.

On uncultivated ground it can be sprayed with 'Tumbleweed' and will succumb after a couple of applications. Give the weedkiller time to take effect, though, and follow the application instructions to the letter. It should be applied in a fine spray on a bright day, and never sprayed until it runs off the leaves. Spring and summer (when plants are growing actively) are the best times to apply.

Where ground elder grows among border plants, overall spraying is not helpful – it will kill the border plants as well as the weed. If infestations are small, paint the leaves of the weed with 'Tumbleweed Gel'. Where outbreaks are severe there's only one thing for it: dig out the cultivated plants in early spring, pull out all the weed from among their roots, and replant them in clean soil while the weedy area is treated with 'Tumbleweed' during the following summer. The cultivated plants can then be replanted in the clean ground in autumn. It's arduous but it's effective.

Among shrubs, ground elder can be wiped out by regular hoeing. It never grows in regularly mown lawns, which shows that it is severely weakened by the removal of top growth.

Bindweed needs to be similarly treated. Couch grass is easier to control since the advent of 'Weed-Out'. This is a selective weedkiller which can be sprayed on to beds and borders where couch grass has infested border plants and shrubs. It will kill off the couch but not the cultivated plants. Spring and early summer are the best times to apply.

Flowerless wisteria

There are hundreds of these all over the country if your letters are anything to go by. For a start, wisterias like sun, so plant them against a south or west-facing wall. They need pruning twice a year; shorten their side-shoots to finger-length in January and shorten those long and questing stems to about a foot (30 cm) in July. Tie in at full length any that you need to extend the plant's territory.

Feed with rose fertiliser in March and again in July, scattering it on the soil around the main stem.

If after three years of this treatment your plant still does not flower, dig it

Ground elder

46

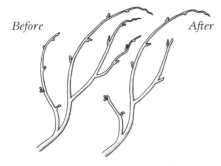

Before   *After*

Pruning wisteria side-shoots in January

up and burn it and plant, instead, a wisteria which has been grafted. Too many wisterias raised from cuttings are shy of flowering. Grafted types (and you can see where the top growth has been grafted on to the fatter rootstock just above the soil level) will flower when only two or three years old.

Green water
Not a disease of sheep but a common complaint of garden pools. The solution is what is known as 'achieving a balance'. The pool should not be in full shade. If in full sun, then a waterlily or two should be planted to protect some of the water's surface from the glare. The pool should not be too shallow; 18 inches (45 cm) is about right.

Plenty of oxygenating plants of the submerged variety should be put in the water, a small clump every 2 feet (60 cm) or so. Never change the water – it will eventually clear after the initial greening that happens whenever a new pool is made.

Brown leaves on house plants
This is almost always caused by dry air, and the letters flood in during November when the central heating has been on for about a month. Spraying the plants with tepid water is time-consuming and damaging to furniture. Instead, stand the plants on a tin tray of gravel which is kept constantly moist. That way they'll be equipped with their own Turkish bath and the browning will stop.

Moss in lawns
Learn to live with it, or see pages 20 and 21. If the lawn looks green, I'd suffer it if I were you!

Soggy roses
In wet weather, many roses have a tendency to turn soggy and brown in the bud. It's a condition known as 'balling' and there's nothing you can do about it except to choose varieties that are resistant to it. Some are more prone to the condition than others. In good summers it's not too much of a problem.

Cats
Other people's cats always come into your garden. Yours will go into other people's. First, provide them with a clump of catmint in which to roll – it will take their minds off scraping up the soil in your seed-beds. Twiggy pea-sticks laid flat over newly sown soil will help to stop them scratching; 9-inch (23-cm) high sticks pushed among prized plants are also said to discourage them.

Among recommendations that viewers have sent me are: curry powder, grated orange and lemon peel, and mothballs – all to be scattered among cherished plants that are being damaged. I've found a water pistol very effective at discouraging them, but my best method has 12 legs. Our three dogs see them off well.

Moles
A real pain in the lawn. If you're surrounded by meadowland, tough luck – they'll always return. You can try pushing paraffin-soaked rags down the molehills, or crushed mothballs; they find the smell of both repellent. Children's windmills stuck in the hills are

47

supposed to send down unpleasant vibrations, as are empty wine bottles sunk into the hills when the wind whistles across their necks.

Some garden centres sell 'mole movers' which are metal spikes that can be pushed into a run. Atop the spike is a plastic box equipped with a battery which sends vibrations down the spike at intervals, scaring off the mole. It would be cheaper, perhaps, to hire the local mole catcher from the council, or to buy a trap and catch Moley in his run. If you're soft-hearted you can always release him into farmland several miles away.

Clematis wilt

For no obvious reason, and when they are in the peak of health, some clematis plants collapse overnight and die. The explanation is the dreaded clematis wilt, but it is seldom fatal. Cut the plant right down to ground level and water the soil with 'Benlate'. Repeat the treatment at monthly intervals and new shoots will eventually grow away from the base.

Birds

Plastic netting is the only fully effective way of preventing birds from demolishing cabbages and stealing strawberries. Fruit bushes such as raspberries should be grown in an impenetrable fruit cage. Black cotton should never be used – all it does is cripple the birds.

Bitch urine on lawns

Bitches in season will burn brown patches on lawns when they squat. As soon as you see them going down, dash out with a bucket of water – not for the dog but for the lawn. Diluted immediately it will not stain. Once the grass has gone brown there's not much you can do except patch it with a spare piece of turf – or wait until it greens up again, which it will do in a few weeks.

Toadstools

Toadstools often pop up on lawns. Usually this is a result of old tree stumps buried below the surface, but they may be caused by fungus disease called fairy rings. Don't try chemical preparations which can be very toxic and are often ineffective. Instead, sweep off the toadstools with a birch broom. It's quick, safe and easy to do.

Woodlice

These little armoured creepy-crawlies are a real pain when they attack seedlings. They occur in cool and shady spots where there's plenty of rubbish for them to feed on. The obvious way of controlling them is to clean up your act and leave less rubbish lying around, but that's often easier said than done – every garden has dirty hedge bottoms and a compost heap.

What you may find helpful are those small blue slug pellets. Woodlice are happy to feed on them and will succumb in the same way as slugs to the poison they contain.

Deer

Gardens that adjoin woodland are frequently used as feeding grounds by red, fallow or roe deer. It's a real delight to see these animals walking across your lawn, but it's heartbreaking to come down in the morning and find that your rose bed has been ravaged overnight so that there's not a bloom in sight. I know the feeling – it's happened to me on more than one occasion.

Different folk come up with different solutions. Some try hanging hairnets full of human hair among the plants. Others suggest that if the tops of fence posts are painted with creosote every four weeks, the scent will deter the deer. I've found that some of the proprietary chemicals sold as deer repellants are quite good, but they do need to be renewed every few weeks,

Busy lizzies in the shade of a tree in my own garden

My own garden
Above *The white bridge in spring*
Right *View up the slope towards the bridge*

Above *Border with patio beyond in Anita Roddick's garden*
Left *Beds edged with box and the gazebo in Sir Hardy Amies's garden*

Above *The designer garden designed and fitted by Bill Wrighton for the* Daytime
Live *programme at Pebble Mill*
Left *Millstone in the water garden I designed for the Chelsea Flower Show*

Pot planted with Helichrysum petiolatum *in my own garden*

and bars of fences and gates repainted with them. The bark of young trees can be protected with spiral plastic rabbit guards which are equally effective with deer.

In truth, the only way of being sure that deer cannot enter your garden is to erect an 8-foot (240-cm) fence around it, but here you're talking mega-bucks to control your mega-bucks and does!

Celandine

A lovely woodland plant which cheers us all up every spring when it erupts with its sheets of yellow flowers. Unfortunately, it doesn't cheer us up when it infests beds and borders. Here it grows thickly enough to smother smaller plants which are trying to grow among it.

'Tumbleweed' will kill it off, but then it will also kill off the plants that grow around it. I find that it's far better to grow taller and more vigorous plants in borders where celandine is a problem, and to pull off some of the foliage to weaken the weed in spring.

The reason for this *laissez-faire* attitude is that in June the celandine dies away completely, and so for at least eight months of the year it is not in evidence. It spreads by means of little tubers – the more you can remove from the soil when you are forking or hoeing, the better, but it always seems to survive!

Leaf browning

Japanese maples, golden-leafed shrubs and other garden plants are sometimes ruined by crisping and browning of the leaves. This state of affairs is most usually brought about by either hot, dry weather, or drying winds. Make sure that the plants are positioned in a sheltered spot, and that they are never allowed to go short of moisture at the roots. Mulching them in spring with manure or pulverised bark will help soil to retain moisture. I've also found that Japanese maples surrounded by cobbles take longer to show the effects of really hot weather.

Browning of conifers

The innermost branches of conifers do turn brown with age, and this is a state of affairs that isn't a problem, so long as the browning can't be seen. When the

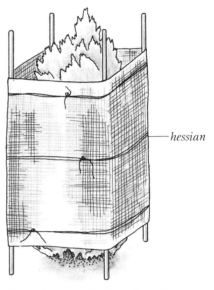

hessian

Protecting a newly planted conifer

browning spreads to the outside of the tree then it is a problem. It can be caused by a number of things, the most common of which is the elevation of the rear leg of a nearby Alsatian. It can also be caused by drying winds and dry soil.

To prevent it happening on newly planted conifers on exposed sites, make sure that the soil remains moist after planting, and protect the newcomers with a wrap of hessian during their first winter. After that they should be capable of sticking up for themselves.

49

GARDEN POOLS

Sooner or later you'll succumb to water. It gives a garden movement, sound and reflection. But a pool can give the gardener a whole new world of problems, though not if it's properly constructed and planted up with a bit of thought. A well-made pool will become the part of the garden to which everyone is drawn.

Spring is the best time to make a pool – between April and June. The first thing to consider is where the pool should go. It needs sun, not shade, so site it in the open. Under trees it will fill with leaves every autumn.

The shape of the pool is up to you, but the bigger it is, the greater your chances of keeping the water clear. As to depth, aim for 1½ feet (45 cm). If it's shallower than 1 foot (30 cm), your pool will heat up too rapidly in summer; if more than 2 feet (60 cm), it will remain cold and the bottom will be thick with mud.

Instead of making the sides of the pool straight, step them so that aquatic plants which enjoy growing in the shallows can be placed, in their special plastic baskets, around the margin of the pool.

Mark out the shape of your pool, either with a trail of sand or with canes and string (if it's a formal shape). Before you dig the hole, work out what you're going to do with the soil. Heaped up at the side of the pool it always looks like a spoil heap, rather than the rock garden you hoped it would. Use it to make up hollow beds and borders, or distribute it evenly on beds and borders over the garden. Alternatively, stack it in a corner as a useful supply of topsoil.

With the hole dug the hardest job is out of the way. In the past, heavy concreting or clay puddling would be the next task, but now there are PVC pool liners to make the job easier. Butyl liners are the longest lasting, but also the most expensive. Sheet polythene is the cheapest but it will last only three or four years in most circumstances. PVC is durable and not overpriced. Use the following sum to calculate the size of liner you need: Length of pool + twice the depth + 2 feet (60 cm) × width of pool + twice depth + 2 feet (60 cm). The extra 2 feet (60 cm) in either direction allows for the liner to be buried well at the edges.

Before putting the liner in place, beat the soil with a spade to bury any sharp stones or pieces of glass that could perforate the liner, and line the entire hole with plenty of newspaper. Stretch the liner over the hole, holding the edges against the ground with a few bricks. Lay a hose-pipe so that it squirts into the centre of the pool, and, as it fills up, ease out any creases in the liner.

When the final water level is reached, switch off the tap and turn your attention to the most important part of the job – the edging. When the pool is finished, no part of the liner should be visible. Use paving slabs for preference, bedding them flat against the earth and tucking the liner underneath them. They should overlap the edge of the pool by a couple of inches (5 cm), and be about an inch (2.5 cm) above the water level. Formal pools can be surrounded by square or rectangular slabs, informal pools by crazy paving.

Use the water as your straight-edge when it comes to getting the paving slabs level. Never attempt to edge your pool before it's been filled with water. If you do, you're bound to find it skew-whiff when you fill it up.

When your pool is finished, leave it

for a couple of weeks before you introduce any plants. Satisfy yourself by planting up around the pool to make it look a part of the garden. Irises look especially good alongside pools, as do hostas and ferns.

After a couple of weeks, aquatic plants can be put in the pool. Small bunches of a submerged oxygenator such as curled pondweed (*Elodea crispa*) can be dropped in at 2-foot (60-cm) intervals, weighted with small pieces of lead. These plants are important as they provide oxygen and help to prevent the water going green.

Marginal aquatic plants can be placed in pots or special plastic planting baskets on the shelves around the edge of the pool where you've created shallows, and those that like deeper water, such as water-lilies, can be submerged in the centre of the pool. Don't drop them into the murky depths straight away; stand their containers on a couple of bricks in the bottom of the pool, and lower them to their final position in a further two weeks' time.

If you buy your aquatic plants in small plastic pots, transfer them to aquatic baskets or larger pots before putting them in the pool. Use ordinary garden soil around their roots rather then potting compost which can foul the water. Spread gravel over the surface of the compost to prevent fish from digging around in the earth.

Avoid at all costs that dreadful floating plant duckweed (lemna). It will take over the surface of the water before you know where you are.

The best regulated of pools turn green a few weeks after being constructed. Be patient. If the submerged oxygenating plants are present and the pool is of the right depth it will eventually clear. A smattering of water-lily leaves helps too, but choose varieties such as 'Froebeli' (rosy red), *Nymphaea odorata minor* (white) and 'Rose Arey' (pink), which are suitable for small pools. No more than a third of the surface of the water should be covered with water-lily pads. Never empty the pool and start again; you'll be back to square one.

Blanketweed, that fine and filamentous green stuff, is easiest to fish out with a wire-toothed rake.

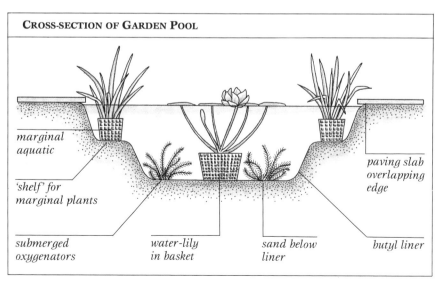

CROSS-SECTION OF GARDEN POOL

marginal aquatic

'shelf' for marginal plants

paving slab overlapping edge

submerged oxygenators

water-lily in basket

sand below liner

butyl liner

51

Within a month of being planted up, your pool can receive its fish. Common or garden goldfish are by far the easiest and most reliable, along with golden orfe which swim just below the surface in shoals. Koi carp are expensive and not to everyone's taste. Give me a fairground goldfish every time! They'll need feeding once a week from April to October, and floating pellets are the easiest thing to use. As far as numbers are concerned, allow 1 square foot (30 sq cm) of pool surface for each fish.

As well as fish, you'll find that dragonflies and damselflies, frogs, toads and newts also make use of your facilities. Great slug-catchers are frogs and toads.

Herons will come too – to eat the fish. A single strand of nylon fishing-line fastened around the pool 6 inches (15 cm) off the ground is a great deterrent to them. Make it thick fishing-line so it can't tangle with the feet of other birds.

All you have to do then is sit back and enjoy your pool. Only in autumn will dead foliage need removing and you can scrape out the bottom and remove any mud every three or four years – but that's a long time off. For now, enjoy it!

Pool plants

Around the shallow edges of the pool, where the water is between 9 inches (23 cm) and 1 foot (30 cm) deep, you can position: sweet flag (acorus), flowering rush (butomus), bog arum (calla), kingcup (caltha), smooth iris (*Iris laevigata*), flag iris (*Iris pseudacorus*), water mint (mentha), bog bean (menyanthes), and water forget-me-not (myosotis).

In the depths will be water-lilies, water hawthorn (aponogeton) and brandy bottle (nuphar). Don't overdo these – you want to be able to see some water.

MILLSTONE FOUNTAIN

Within the designer garden at *Daytime Live* we built a millstone fountain like the one in my own garden. This little beauty can be built by a couple of strong men in an afternoon and is a real eye-catcher. It offers the sound, movement and reflective properties of water, without any depth of water to be a danger to children.

You'll need: one millstone or grindstone about 2 feet (60 cm) across (scour junk shops, builders' yards and farm sales); one circular black plastic domestic water tank (the kind that's

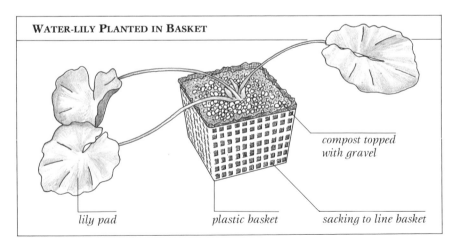

WATER-LILY PLANTED IN BASKET

lily pad *plastic basket* *sacking to line basket*

compost topped with gravel

52

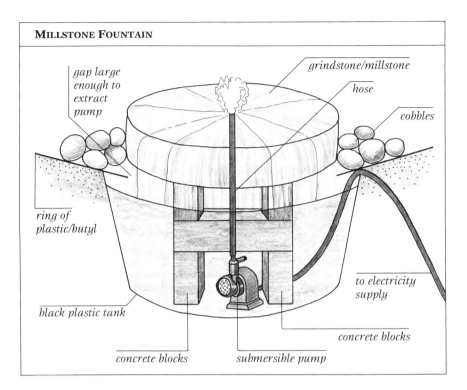

gap large enough to extract pump

grindstone/millstone

hose

cobbles

ring of plastic/butyl

to electricity supply

black plastic tank

concrete blocks

concrete blocks

submersible pump

used in your loft); six concrete building blocks; one submersible pump plus cable and a short length of hose; one Polo-mint-shaped piece of polythene; some cobbles and a little quick-setting cement.

Dig a hole in the ground to accommodate the tank (the hardest part of the job). Sink the tank into the hole and make sure it is level. Use the six concrete building blocks stacked on top of one another in twos, like a tower of dominoes, and then put the polythene ring in position. It should overlap the rim of the tank by 2 or 3 inches (5–7.5 cm) all round. Put the pump, with the short length of hose, in position and heave the millstone into place. Check that it is central and level (use a spirit level).

Make sure that the gap between the millstone and the rim of the tank is large enough to get the pump in and out to clean the filter from time to time. Pass the hose up through the hole in the millstone and cement it into place.

Arrange cobbles around the edge of the millstone to cover the gap, and then fill the tank with water. The cable for the pump (preferably armoured) should be buried 18 inches (45 cm) deep in the soil and the plug at the end should be fitted with an earth leakage circuit breaker.

When the pump is switched on, water will come up through the hole in the centre of the stone, run over its surface, and be directed back down into the tank by the polythene. All your fountain needs is an occasional topping up to replace evaporation. Hostas, irises and other flowering and foliage plants can be grouped around the cobbles. They'll look terrific!

53

ROCK GARDENING

The last thing you need to grow rock-plants is rock. They'll grow in any soil that's well drained, provided they have plenty of light. In their native habitats, most alpine plants grow between rocks or over rocks, but it's what their roots are growing in that's important.

A rock garden might seem the obvious place to grow them, but they are also at home at the front of flower beds and borders where many of them make great edgers; they look good on top of soil-filled retaining walls, they thrive in sinks and troughs, but most especially they look good in beds devoted to themselves.

These beds can be raised off the ground with low brick or stone retaining walls to a height of 18 inches (45 cm) (advisable where soil is heavy and poorly drained) or at ground level. Many are happy in chalky soils, and almost any soil can be made more to their liking by the addition of some peat, about a bucketful to the square yard (sq m), and sharp grit (applied at the same rate). Make sure your bed is in full sun and your alpines will never look back.

Pot-grown alpines can be planted at any time of year, spacing them from 9 to 18 inches (23–45 cm) apart, depending on their tendency to spread. Once planted, the soil can be covered with 1 inch (2.5 cm) of washed pea shingle or gravel). It shows off the plants to perfection, prevents them from being splashed by mud, helps to keep in moisture and to keep down weeds, and it gives them good drainage around their stems. Whenever you need to plant something new, just scrape away the gravel, plant it and push the gravel back afterwards.

All right, so you'd like a bit of rock. There are many types to choose from, but try to select something that will look at home in your area. Sandstone, limestone and assorted gritstones are all suitable and are sold by the ton. A ton does not go very far. Use your rocks to best effect by burying only a quarter or a third of them for stability, and allowing the majority of the stone to show. Lay each rock so that any visible lines or strata are running horizontally (not vertically) and sloping backwards slightly. That way the rocks will look more natural than if they are stuck in any old how like plums in a pudding.

In backyards and patio gardens, alpines can be grown in sinks and troughs. Make an artificial 'stone' trough out of a white porcelain butler's sink (see page 25), or use the real thing.

PLACING OF ROCK IN A ROCK GARDEN

The strata run slightly backwards and all in the same direction

54

Most alpines and rock-plants are at their best in spring and early summer, so it follows that they are usually planted in March and April so that they can be enjoyed in their first season. Extend the season of interest by planting dwarf bulbs such as *Iris reticulata*, snowdrops and botanical tulips among them, and by adding a few dwarf conifers for year-round form. Heathers with coloured foliage and flowers that can appear at any time of year (according to variety) help as well, but too many of them can be overpowering.

As a race, rock-plants are undemanding. A sprinkling of blood, bone and fishmeal on the gravel around them each spring will prove to be quite enough in the way of annual nourishment, and any faded stems can be snipped back in autumn. There's a host of plants to choose from, suiting different places.

Rock-plants for rapid cover
Acaena, bugle (ajuga), snow-in-summer (cerastium), *Genista sagittalis*, *Geranium sanguineum*, rock roses (helianthemum), *Iberis sempervirens*, *Polygonum affine*, mossy saxifrages, thymes (thymus).

Rock-plants for sink gardens
Rock jasmine (androsace), thrift (armeria), pinks (dianthus), gentians, edelweiss (leontopodium), lewisia, encrusted saxifrages, houseleeks (sempervivum), thymes (thymus), and the Noah's ark juniper (*Juniperus communis* 'Compressa').

Rock-plants for retaining walls
Arabis, aubrieta, bellflowers (campanula), snow-in-summer (cerastium), *Genista sagittalis*, rock roses (helianthemum), *Iberis sempervirens*, lewisia, lithospermum, alpine poppies (papaver), *Polygonum affine*, soapwort (saponaria), saxifrages, stonecrops (sedum), houseleeks (sempervivum).

Rock-plants in paving
Patios are often thought of as places for tubs, troughs and pots, but not as homes for alpines which can grow in crevices between the paving stones. But many rock-plants are happy when their roots can seek out the cool, moist earth below a paving slab, and if the plant is a ground hugger it can decorate an otherwise bald area to great effect.

Even better are cushion-forming and creeping plants with aromatic leaves that release their scent when crushed – plants like thyme and the lower-growing grey artemisias (though, to be fair, the soft leaves of artemisia are best brushed past rather than squashed).

The best time to plant is early spring, so that the plants can grow away rapidly in the warmer weather ahead. Water each plant well in its pot and then use a long, thin trowel to scoop out a hole between the slabs. Push the root-ball into place, surround it with more soil and then water the plant in.

As well as being planted individually in small crevices, rock-plants can also be planted in groups in areas of well-drained soil that are left at intervals among the paving. If the soil is topdressed with sharp grit or gravel after planting, not only are the plants protected from mud splashing but they are also surrounded by a surface that offers a pleasant contrast to the flat stonework. Pebbles or small pieces of rock can also be placed among them, but, just a minute, before we know where we are we'll have a fully fledged rock garden on our hands.

Plants for paving
Arabis, thrift (armeria), aubrieta, bellflower (campanula), snow-in-summer (cerastium), pinks (dianthus), rock roses (helianthemum), alpine poppy (papaver), pratia, *Polygonum affine*, sagina, soapwort (saponaria), saxifrages, stonecrops (sedum), houseleeks (sempervivum), violas.

PLANTS FOR DIFFICULT PLACES

I've never met a gardener yet who doesn't think his patch of earth is a problem plot. Everyone claims to have the worst soil in Britain, and the worst garden when it comes to aspect and microclimate.

The truth of the matter is that we all have patches in our garden that give us trouble. They may be riddled with tree roots, or in deep shade; the soil might be chalky or badly drained. When three or four different plants have been tried there you might feel inclined to concrete the lot. Stay your hand; try to find plants that are naturally equipped to thrive in your problem patches and they may ease your heartache. Here's a guide to plants that thrive where others won't.

Plants for shade

Shrubs: bamboo (arundinaria), spotted laurel (aucuba), barberry (berberis), box (buxus), camellia, hazel (corylus), cotoneaster, *Euonymus fortunei*, false castor oil (fatsia), ivy (hedera), rose of Sharon (hypericum), holly (ilex), juniper, laurel (*Prunus laurocerasus*), mahonia, pernettya, flame of the forest (pieris), rhododendron, elder (sambucus), sarcococca, skimmia, evergreen viburnums, periwinkle (vinca).

Border perennials: bear's breech (acanthus), monkshood (aconitum), bugle (ajuga), lady's mantle (alchemilla), alkanet (anchusa), anemone, columbine (aquilegia), arum, astilbe, astrantia, elephant's ears (bergenia), brunnera, lily of the valley (convallaria), montbretia (crocosmia), dicentra, foxglove (digitalis), bishop's hat (epimedium), euphorbia, ferns, hardy geraniums, glyceria, gunnera, hellebores, day lilies (hemerocallis),

heuchera, hosta, dead-nettle (lamium), meconopsis, monkey flower (mimulus), Jacob's ladder (polemonium), Solomon's seal (polygonatum), knotweed (polygonum), primula, lungwort (pulmonaria), rodgersia, lamb's ears (stachys), viola.

Rodgersia pinnata

Plants for dry soil

All should be watered well until their roots are established; after that they are well adapted to fend for themselves.

Shrubs: bamboo (arundinaria), barberry (berberis), buddleia, box (buxus), blue spiraea (caryopteris), sun rose (cistus), hazel (corylus), cotoneaster, broom (cytisus), deutzia, elaeagnus, escallonia, euonymus, genista, heather, hebe, ivy (hedera), hibiscus, rose of Sharon (hypericum), tree mallow (lavatera), mahonia, myrtle, olearia, osmanthus, mock orange (philadelphus), Jerusalem sage

56

(phlomis), pittosporum, potentilla, sumach (rhus), flowering currant (ribes), rosemary, rue (ruta), lavender cotton (santolina), sarcococca, skimmia, spiraea, tamarisk, *Viburnum tinus*, periwinkle (vinca), yucca.

Border perennials: bear's breech (acanthus), yarrow (achillea), agapanthus, lady's mantle (alchemilla), Peruvian lily (alstroemeria), artemisia, astrantia, ballota, elephant's ears (bergenia), cornflower (centaurea), valerian (centranthus), lily of the valley (convallaria), montbretia (crocosmia), foxglove (digitalis), globe thistle (echinops), sea holly (eryngium), euphorbia, gaillardia, hardy geraniums, some irises, red-hot poker (kniphofia), dead-nettle (lamium), liatris, flax (linum), catmint (nepeta), evening primrose (oenothera), peony, oriental poppy, penstemon, phlox, potentilla, salvia, sedum, veronica.

Plants for chalky soil

Shrubs: snowy mespilus (amelanchier), bamboo (arundinaria), spotted laurel (aucuba), barberry (berberis), buddleia, box (buxus), blue spiraea (caryopteris), Mexican orange blossom (choisya), sun rose (cistus), dogwood (*Cornus alba*), hazel (corylus), smoke bush (cotinus), cotoneaster, *Daphne mezereum*, deutzia, elaeagnus, escallonia, euonymus, false castor oil (fatsia), forsythia, fuchsia, heather (*Erica carnea* varieties), hebe, ivy (hedera), hibiscus, hydrangea, rose of Sharon (hypericum), holly (ilex), juniper, lavender, tree mallow (lavatera), mahonia, myrtle, olearia, tree peony, mock orange (philadelphus), Jerusalem sage (phlomis), pittosporum, potentilla, flowering currant (ribes), rosemary, rue (ruta), willow (salix), elder (sambucus), lavender cotton (santolina), sarcococca, skimmia, lilac (syringa), tamarisk, periwinkle (vinca), weigela, yucca.

Elephant's ears (bergenia)

Border perennials: bear's breech (acanthus), yarrow (achillea), monkshood (aconitum), agapanthus, bugle (ajuga), lady's mantle (alchemilla), allium, Peruvian lily (alstroemeria), alkanet (anchusa), anemone, columbine (aquilegia), artemisia, arum, aster, astilbe, astrantia, ballota, elephant's ears (bergenia), bellflower (campanula), cornflower (centaurea), valerian (centranthus), chrysanthemum, lily of the valley (convallaria), delphinium, pinks and carnations (dianthus), dicentra, foxglove (digitalis), leopard's bane (doronicum), globe thistle (echinops), bishop's hat (epimedium), foxtail lily (eremurus), sea holly (eryngium), euphorbia, gaillardia, hardy geraniums, geum, glyceria, gypsophila, helenium, hellebores, day lilies (hemerocallis), heuchera, hosta, irises, red-hot poker (kniphofia), dead-nettle (lamium), liatris, flax (linum), lysimachia, monkey flower (mimulus), bergamot (monarda), catmint (nepeta), evening primrose (oenothera), peony, poppy, penstemon, phlox, Jacob's ladder (polemonium), Solomon's seal (polygonatum), knotweed (polygonum), potentilla, lungwort (pulmonaria), rodgersia, rudbeckia, salvia, scabious, sedum, verbascum, veronica, viola.

Plants for clay soil

Shrubs: maple (acer), snowy mespilus (amelanchier), bamboo (arundinaria), spotted laurel (aucuba), barberry (berberis), buddleia, box (buxus), Mexican orange blossom (choisya), hazel (corylus), smoke bush (cotinus), cotoneaster, broom (cytisus), deutzia, elaeagnus, escallonia, euonymus, false castor oil (fatsia), forsythia, fuchsia, genista, witch hazel (hamamelis), heathers, hebe, ivy (hedera), hibiscus, hydrangea, rose of Sharon (hypericum), holly (ilex), juniper, lavender, magnolia, mahonia, olearia, pernettya, mock orange (philadelphus), pittosporum, potentilla, rhododendron, sumach (rhus), flowering currant (ribes), willow (salix), elder (sambucus), sarcococca, skimmia, spiraea, lilac (syringa), tamarisk, viburnum, periwinkle (vinca), weigela.

Jerusalem sage (phlomis)

Border perennials: bear's breeches (acanthus), yarrow (achillea), monkshood (aconitum), bugle (ajuga), lady's mantle (alchemilla), hollyhock (althaea), alkanet (anchusa), anemone, columbine (aquilegia), arum, aster, astilbe, astrantia, elephant's ears (bergenia), cornflower (centaurea), chrysanthemum, coreopsis, mont-

bretia (crocosmia), delphinium, foxglove (digitalis), leopard's bane (doronicum), globe thistle (echinops), bishop's hat (epimedium), hardy geraniums, geum, glyceria, helenium, hellebores, day lilies (hemerocallis), heuchera, hosta, iris, red-hot poker (kniphofia), dead-nettle (lamium), lupin, lysimachia, mallow (malva), monkey flower (mimulus), bergamot (monarda), peony, phlox, Jacob's ladder (polemonium), knotweed (polygonum), primula, lungwort (pulmonaria), ornamental rhubarb (rheum), rodgersia, rudbeckia, scabious, sedum, verbascum, veronica, viola.

Plants for coastal gardens

Shrubs: bamboo (arundinaria), spotted laurel (aucuba), barberry (berberis), buddleia, blue spiraea (caryopteris), Mexican orange blossom (choisya), sun rose (cistus), cotoneaster, broom (cytisus), elaeagnus, escallonia, false castor oil (fatsia), fuchsia, genista, hebe, ivy (hedera), hibiscus, hydrangea, rose of Sharon (hypericum), holly (ilex), juniper, lavender, tree mallow (lavatera), myrtle, olearia, Jerusalem sage (phlomis), pittosporum, potentilla, flowering currant (ribes), rosemary, elder (sambucus), lavender cotton (santolina), skimmia, spiraea, tamarisk, weigela, yucca.

Border perennials: yarrow (achillea), agapanthus, Peruvian lily (alstroemeria), anemone, artemisia, elephant's ears (bergenia), cornflower (centaurea), valerian (centranthus), chrysanthemum, sea kale (crambe), montbretia (crocosmia), pinks and carnations (dianthus), globe thistle (echinops), sea holly (eryngium), euphorbia, hardy geraniums, gypsophila, heuchera, iris, red-hot poker (kniphofia), evening primrose (oenothera), penstemon, knotweed (polygonum), potentilla, salvia, scabious, sedum, tradescantia, veronica.

Plants for cold and exposed gardens
Shrubs: barberry (berberis), buddleia, hazel (corylus), smoke bush (cotinus), cotoneaster, deutzia, elaeagnus, euonymus, forsythia, witch hazel (hamamelis), hawthorn (crataegus), heathers, ivy (hedera), holly (ilex), juniper, *Mahonia aquifolium*, pernettya, mock orange (philadelphus), potentilla, flowering currant (ribes), willow (salix), elder (sambucus), skimmia, spiraea, lilac (syringa), tamarisk, viburnum, periwinkle (vinca), weigela.

Variegated periwinkle
(*Vinca major* 'Elegantissima')

Border perennials: worth trying a wide range. Most die down in winter when the wind and weather are at their worst and emerge unscathed the following spring. Very tall plants such as lupins and delphiniums may be unsuitable.

IMPROVING PROBLEM PLACES
It's always worth remembering that problem places can almost always be improved to give the plants that are being grown there a far better chance of succeeding. If the area is shady, can more light be let in? This does not mean that trees should be butchered, but it is often possible to lighten the darkness underneath them by care-

fully thinning out the overhead canopy. This means removing a few of the branches completely so that the overall shape of the tree is retained, but more light is admitted between the branches.

If soil is in poor shape, being either dust-dry or waterlogged, an improvement in condition will make the cultivation of a wider range of plants more possible. Clay soil can be improved by adding bulky organic matter such as well-rotted garden compost or animal manure, and also sharp grit, which is much longer lasting in its effect.

The adding of organic matter will also benefit sandy soils, which need more regular feeding than ordinary soils due to the fact that water washes nutrients out of them very quickly.

Chalky soils are far less of a problem than you might think. True enough, in very shallow soils over chalk many plants become stunted and pale of leaf. But even here they will often do well if a large enough hole can be dug for them in the first place, and plenty of organic matter then worked in. Steer clear of the obvious lime-haters like aganas, rhododendrons and camelias, pieris and some heathers; most other plants will be happy. Like sandy soil, chalky soil needs feeding regularly, and if plants are given an annual sprinkling of blood, bone and fishmeal on the soil around their roots, and an occasional mulch with well-rotted manure or garden compost, they need never look back.

Very windy sites can be made more amenable to plant growth by planting windbreaks such as hawthorn or *Cupressus macrocarpa*. Alternatively, you can erect windbreaks, and these should filter the wind rather than attempt to stop it dead (slatted fencing rather than solid panels). Windbreaks are also vital by the sea to cut down salty winds. Given a head start, most plants will do their best to succeed.

CLIMBERS AND WALL PLANTS

There's nothing quite so disappointing as a bare house wall or garden fence. Naked brick or woodwork simply cries out for climbing plants. Don't believe all you hear about climbers pulling mortar out of walls and causing rising damp; if the right plants are chosen and planted in the proper way, your house will not come to any harm.

By the right plants I mean shrubs that climb or scramble, or which simply enjoy being planted where the wall can offer them protection that they would not receive in the open garden. Trees are not wall plants and should never be planted nearer to houses than 15 feet (4.5 m), and then they should be small trees, not monsters like willow, poplar and sycamore which are efficient foundation lifters.

Never plant self-clingers such as ivy directly on to pebbledash; they may, in future years when they are weighty, peel the stuff from the wall in one huge sheet. Neither should you pile soil up high against the house wall so that the damp-proof course is bridged. Keep the soil below the damp-proof course and there will be no problem with rising damp.

Climbers can also be used to add height to gardens where trees are too large and gloom-inducing. Let them scramble up tripods of rustic poles, or over arches and pergolas (a series of linked arches). Colonnades (vertical poles linked by swags of rope) are good for supporting climbing roses and clematis.

Against a house wall or fence, some climbers will shin up on their own. Ivy has aerial roots that cling, and Virginia creeper uses sticky pads. Other plants have twining stems, leaf stalks or tendrils that need something to cling to other than a flat surface. For these, by far the simplest support system is horizontal strands of plastic-coated wire held at 18-inch (45-cm) intervals with masonry nails hammered into the brickwork (galvanised nails for wooden fences). Stems can be tied in where necessary to encourage upward and sideways travel.

Where self-clingers are reluctant to cling, try painting the surface of the wall or fence with a mixture of manure and water – it encourages closer contact!

The soil at the bottom of a fence or wall is almost always on the dry side. Beef it up with plenty of organic matter before you plant. Well-rotted manure or garden compost is best, but peat with blood, bone and fishmeal added is a decent substitute.

You can plant at any time of year from containers, and every plant will benefit from being mulched with manure or compost after planting. Keep a hose handy during the first year of establishment to make sure the soil never dries out.

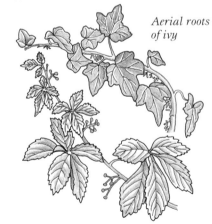

Aerial roots of ivy

Suckers of Virginia creeper

Clematis especially appreciate a few pieces of broken paving slab placed on the soil around their stem, which keeps them cool at the roots.

All climbers enjoy food from time to time. Get into the habit of giving them rose fertiliser in March and again in July. It promotes flowering and lustrous foliage, regardless of whether the plants are roses or not.

Pruning varies from climber to climber, but remember that you are trying to keep a well-spaced framework of flowering shoots, rather than a dense thicket of flowerless greenery.

Wisterias are pruned in January – shortening side-shoots to finger length – and again in July, cutting back those snaking shoots to about a foot (30 cm).

Clematis are pruned in February, cutting back to where downy buds can be seen to be emerging. Only *Clematis montana* and *C. macropetala* are pruned after flowering by thinning out their growths.

Remember that, in general, the harder you prune, the more growth will result.

Climbers and shrubs for walls of different aspects

North-facing walls: camellia, Japanese quince or japonica (chaenomeles), clematis, *Cotoneaster horizontalis*,

Twining leaf stalks of clematis

garrya, ivy (hedera), climbing hydrangea, winter jasmine, Virginia creeper (parthenocissus), Russian vine (*Polygonum baldschuanicum*), firethorn (pyracantha), rose 'Mermaid'.

South- or west-facing walls: *Abutilon vitifolium*, *Actinidia kolomikta*, camellia, carpenteria, Californian lilac (ceanothus), clematis, *Cotoneaster horizontalis*, Moroccan broom (*Cytisus battandieri*), fremontodendron, garrya, ivy (hedera), climbing hydrangea, winter jasmine and white-flowered jas-

Spiralling stem of honeysuckle

Tendrils of sweet pea

mine, sweet peas, everlasting peas (lathyrus), lemon-scented verbena (lippia), honeysuckle (lonicera), *Magnolia grandiflora*, Virginia creeper (parthenocissus), passion flower (passiflora), Russian vine (*Polygonum baldschuanicum*), firethorn (pyracantha), fuchsia-flowered gooseberry (*Ribes speciosum*), vines (vitis), wisteria.

East-facing walls: japonica (chaenomeles), clematis, *Cotoneaster horizontalis*, garrya, ivy (hedera), hop (humulus), climbing hydrangea, winter jasmine, everlasting pea (lathyrus), Virginia creeper (parthenocissus), Russian vine (*Polygonum baldschuanicum*), firethorn (pyracantha).

61

SOME FOR THE POT

There's not really room in this little book to tackle vegetables in detail, and insufficient room for vegetables is often the problem in small gardens. The answer is to squeeze vegetables into other parts of the garden where they can earn their keep as attractive garden plants as well as nourishing fodder.

Now nobody is going to tell you that there's anything artistic about a Brussels sprout plant. Crisp and succulent its crop may be but your heart will never miss a beat when you view it as part of your herbaceous border. But other vegetables were more kindly treated by nature.

Take Swiss chard. If you've never grown this vegetable then I urge you to try it. It's sometimes sold as leaf beet, and, though that's a title guaranteed to be a turn-off, the plant itself is a stunner. It has fat leaf stalks of creamy white, and oval leaves of shiny green with deep veining. In the form called ruby or rhubarb chard the leaf stalks are rich rosy red. You can eat the leaves like spinach and the leaf stalks can be boiled like celery – two vegetables for the price of one and an attractive plant, to boot.

Try growing it among lettuces. Butterhead varieties or crisphead types like 'Webb's Wonderful' can be as bold as a hosta in a border, but for me the foliage lettuce *par excellence* is 'Salad Bowl'. It's lime green, frilly and can be sown thinly and never subsequently thinned, except to eat. 'Lollo Rossa' is similar but flushed with crimson. With Swiss chard used among them as 'dot' plants they look amazingly swish. Try ditching the lobelia and alyssum one year and replacing them with 'Salad Bowl' or even parsley.

Climbing plants can be used to give height to small gardens where trees are out of the question. Grow them up tripods of canes or bean poles and they make a flat site far more interesting.

Sweet peas are a popular choice, but use runner beans as well and you'll not only have flowers (red in 'Scarlet Emperor', white in 'Mergoles' and pink in 'Sunset'), but a hefty crop of edible pods as well.

Purple-podded peas are real eye-catchers when grown up clumps of brushwood – their flowers are followed by a dusky purple crop of pods. Like the beans, they are gluttons for food and water.

Sword-like leaves in your borders can be provided by onions or leeks, and if you leave leeks in position, or transplant them, for a second year, they'll produce tall flower stalks topped by lilac-pink orbs of bloom. At the back of a border they look good towering over variegated grasses.

Beetroot looks good in and among lettuces, in the same way as Swiss chard, and cabbages make excellent focal points at the ends of beds and borders. Ornamental cabbages, with leaves veined and flushed with purple, pink or white, are real stunners and supposedly edible (though I've never been able to bring myself to cut one!). Grow them as single specimens in large clay flower pots as well as in the garden. They are great patio plants.

As a contrast to bolder leaves, try a patch of feathery carrots. And further back in the border, a small plantation of curly kale – 18 inches (45 cm) high with frothy leaves – looks terrific.

Bold-leafed grasses are revered by plantsmen because they offer good screening material for the compost heap and variety in terms of plant form. But there's one good grass that

There's such a wide range of vegetable varieties offered for sale that it pays to know which are really worth growing. Here's a list of my tried and tested favourites.

Globe artichoke – 'Gros Vert de Laon'
Jerusalem artichoke – 'Fuseau'
Asparagus – 'Lucullus'
Aubergine – 'Long Purple'
Broad bean – 'Bonny Lad'
French bean – 'The Prince'
Runner bean – 'Enorma'
Beetroot – 'Boltardy'
Broccoli – 'Early Purple'
Brussels sprout – 'Peer Gynt'
Cabbage, early summer – 'Hispi'
   summer – 'Wiam'
   winter – 'Celtic'
   spring – 'April'
Calabrese – 'Corvet'
Capsicum (peppers) – 'Worldbeater'
Carrot – 'Favourite'
Cauliflower, summer – 'Snowball'
   autumn – 'Barrier Reef'
   winter – 'Snow's Winter White'

Celeriac – 'Alabaster'
Celery – 'Giant White'
Courgette – 'Zucchini'
Cucumber (greenhouse) – 'Femdan'
   (ridge) – 'Kyoto'
Endive – 'Green Curled' or 'Moss Curled'
Kale – 'Dwarf Green Curled'
Kohl rabi – 'Raoul'
Leek – 'Musselburgh'
Lettuce – 'Webb's Wonderful'
Marrow – 'Green Bush'
Onion – 'Ailsa Craig'
Parsnip – 'Hollow Crown Improved'
Pea – 'Hurst Green Shaft'
Potato – 'Foremost'
Radish – 'Cherry Belle'
Rhubarb – 'Champagne'
Spinach, summer – 'Norvak'
   winter – 'Longstanding Prickly'
Swede – 'Marian'
Sweet corn – 'John Innes Hybrid'
Swiss chard – silver or seakale (green) and ruby or rhubarb (red)
Tomato – 'Alicante'
Turnip – 'Snowball'

---

carries a crop as well – sweet corn. It's always recommended that sweet corn is planted in blocks, rather than single rows, to ensure adequate pollination and full cobs, but there's no reason why you shouldn't shake the plants at flowering time to give them a hand with fruiting if all you can fit in is a single row. Warmth and shelter suits them best; cold, exposed districts are not to their liking.

By far the best screening for any compost heap comes from the Jerusalem artichoke. Plant the tubers in early spring and they'll send up a forest of hairy stems and leaves fully 8 feet (2.5 m) tall. The tuberous roots can be dug up and cooked in autumn and winter and they make the most delicious soup, even if they are a pain in the neck to peel.

We are now left with the aristocrat, the globe artichoke. Few people know how to cook them properly, and even fewer know how to eat them. But master both techniques and you can enjoy this gourmet feast on your plate, and as a statuesque plant in the border. It sends up a fountain of finely cut, grey-green leaves through which push up the flowerheads. Cut them before you can see the flower colour in the centre if you want to eat them. If not, let their huge purple thistle-heads open and add them to your list of ornamental vegetables.

HOUSE PLANTS

Even really reluctant gardeners can be persuaded to grow a house plant or two. The trouble is that more often than not they treat them like pieces of furniture. Now while your Chippendale commode might have been happy for a couple of centuries with an annual application of beeswax and a weekly flick over with a feather duster, these are not conditions guaranteed to promote longevity in house plants.

Those that don't die of neglect may be killed with kindness. There are gardeners who think that house plants need dowsing with water every day. Only Christmas azaleas fall into that category; the rest need water when they are thirsty, just like people.

Watering
If the compost in the pot feels like a freshly wrung out flannel it is moist. That is all any plant needs. Don't apply water.

If the compost in the pot feels dry to the touch – just a trifle dusty – it's dry and the plant needs watering. Apply enough water to the compost so that some comes out of the drainage holes in the base of the pot. Don't leave the plant standing in water for more than half an hour or its roots may rot.

It follows that plants will dry out more quickly in summer than in winter, so they need more water between May and September than they do between October and April.

Ferns, Christmas azaleas and umbrella grass can be kept moist at all times – they really hate dry compost.

Only when a plant cannot be watered from above due to its having a compost-hugging rosette of leaves – a common occurrence with African violets and cyclamen – should it be watered from below. Stand the plant in a bowl of water for half an hour and, after that time, tip out what has not been absorbed.

Feeding
Because their roots are restricted inside the pot, house plants rely on you totally when it comes to food. Give foliage house plants dilute liquid feed once a fortnight from May to September. Flowering pot plants should be watered at the same time and frequency with dilute liquid tomato fertiliser. It works wonders on flowerless African violets.

Pot plants that flower at Christmas should be fed fortnightly when in bud and in bloom.

Light
Most foliage house plants thrive in good indirect light – that's the kind you get about three or four feet (90–120 cm) from a window. Flowering pot plants tend to enjoy being right on the windowsill where it's brighter.

For shady corners of a room, plain green house plants are the most reliable (see the list of plants for shady corners), but where you can't read a telephone directory at arm's length, it's too dark for anything except plastic tulips.

No-go areas
Don't put any plant near to a radiator, on top of a television set or in a howling draught. Don't sandwich plants between the curtains and the window at night – it can be a frost trap.

Humidity
By far the biggest problem with house plants is browning of the leaves. It usually happens when the central heating

House plant on gravel tray

is switched on in autumn and is caused by dry air. Remedy the problem by standing each plant on a plate or tray of gravel which is kept moist. As the water evaporates, the plant's leaves will be surrounded by humid air.

Spraying with a hand-mister is sometimes recommended, but it is time consuming and effective only in the short term, and can result in damaged furniture.

Temperature
Don't alter your way of living; instead, choose plants that will fit into your way of life and the temperatures in your rooms. Some plants are naturally suited to centrally-heated homes; others prefer cool rooms. The lists offer helpful suggestions.

Buying house plants
Buy from a nursery, garden centre or chain store where the plants are fresh and look healthy. Don't buy from freez-

ing pavement displays. Only in summer are the plants offered for sale ourdoors likely to reach you without catching a chill.

Check that the compost in the pot is moist, that it hasn't shrunk away from the pot, and that the plant is bushy and free from pests and diseases.

Potting on
A couple of years after you've bought them, most house plants will be ready for a larger container. Spring is the best time for repotting. Choose a pot that's 2 inches (5 cm) larger in diameter than the existing pot (rather more if the pot is huge). Use John Innes No. 2 potting compost or a peat-based compost (which doesn't need to be firmed quite so much). Water the plant before it is potted on, and water it afterwards to settle the compost into place. Feeding will be unnecessary for a couple of months after potting.

Cleaning
Just like the Chippendale commode, house plants get dusty. If the muck is not removed from their leaves they'll look dull and lifeless, and their rate of growth will slow down. Shiny-leaved plants can be sponged with kitchen roll dipped in a mixture of equal parts milk and water (it gives them a slight gloss but nothing too flashy).

Hairy-leaved plants, such as African violets, are best flicked over with a dry paintbrush.

Shaping up
Never be afraid to pinch out the shoot tips to make a plant more bushy, and always pick off dead leaves and faded flowers. Not only do they look unsightly, but they can also spread disease.

Pests and diseases
Greenfly can be controlled by spraying with a specific aphicide such as 'Rapid

Greenfly Killer' and whitefly, mealy bugs and scale insects (little brown legless jobs) by spraying with 'Tumblebug'. Fungus diseases such as mildew can be controlled by spraying with 'Tumbleblite'.

Don't spray your plants in the sitting room – take them outside the back door, spray them and bring them back inside.

FINDING THE RIGHT PLANT

When you've a spot you want to fill with a plant, find out first which plants will do well in that particular situation. Here's a guide to what will be happy where.

Windowsills

Azalea, flame nettle (coleus), cyclamen, Venus' fly trap (dionaea), fuchsia, ivy (hedera), busy lizzie (impatiens), geranium (pelargonium), primula, African violet (saintpaulia), mother-in-law's tongue (sansevieria), Christmas cactus (schlumbergera), cineraria (senecio), winter cherry (solanum), wandering sailor (tradescantia), zebrina.

Cool rooms 10–16°C (50–60°F)

Azalea, slipper flower (calceolaria), chrysanthemum, cyclamen (hates heat and overwatering), fat-headed lizzie (fatshedera), false castor oil (fatsia), ivy (hedera), primula, cineraria (senecio).

Warm rooms 18–24°C (65–75°F)

Zebra plant (aphelandra), begonia, Joseph's coat (codiaeum), dumb cane (dieffenbachia), dragon tree (dracaena), poinsettia (euphorbia), rubber plant and weeping fig (ficus), palms (howea), Swiss cheese plant (monstera), peperomia, sweetheart plant (philodendron), aluminium plant (pilea), grape ivy (rhoicissus), African violet (saintpaulia), mother-in-law's tongue (sansevieria), gloxinia (sinningia), stephanotis, yucca.

Shady corners

Maidenhair fern (adiantum), asparagus fern, aspidistra, bird's-nest fern (asplenium), kangaroo vine (cissus), fat-headed lizzie (fatshedera), false castor oil (fatsia), prayer plant (maranta), peperomia, sweetheart plant (philodendron), aluminium plant (pilea), stag's-horn fern (platycerium), grape ivy (rhoicissus), mother-in-law's tongue (sansevieria).

BOTTLE GARDENS AND TERRARIUMS

There's a great craze at the moment for terrariums – those little glass greenhouses that adorn coffee tables until their inmates turn brown and cause them to be relegated to the spare bedroom. They're really just a flashy version of the bottle garden and both can be put together and looked after in just the same way.

What plants like about these containers is their ability to keep the atmosphere moist and prevent drying of the foliage. Sadly, though, some terrariums are made on economic lines and only half glazed, which means that they lack the advantageous properties of glass (moisture retention) but are equipped with its disadvantages (the ability to increase heat and scorch

Prayer plant (maranta)

66

leaves). That doesn't mean to say that bottle gardens and terrariums should be kept completely closed up; that would increase condensation and make seeing the plants more difficult. What needs to be achieved is a balance: the retention of humidity and the circulation of a little air. And that's just what you get if the stopper is left off the bottle garden, or a small ventilator is built into the terrarium.

Choose plants for these containers carefully. It's tempting to plant tradescantia and 'mind-your-own-business', but the moment your back is turned they'll swamp the rest of the inmates. Pick house plants that are naturally small and which have a slow rate of growth. That way they'll be happy in the bottle garden or terrarium for a long while and save you the bother of having to replant it every few weeks or at the very least make forays into it with a machete.

Try chamaedorea (a miniature palm), creeping fig, prayer plant (maranta), peperomias, pileas, selaginellas, Venus' fly-traps and even a small-leafed ivy which is easy to snip once it puts on too much stem. African violets (saintpaulias) are tempting, but their faded flowers look a mess and can often spread fungal infection to the leaves. It is best to steer clear of flowering plants.

In the bottom of the container spread ½ inch (12 mm) of gravel topped by ½ inch (12 mm) crushed charcoal (in deep bottles make each layer 1 inch (2.5 cm) deep). Over these drainage layers, which are designed to prevent waterlogging of the compost, you'll need 3 inches (7.5 cm) of compost such as John Innes No. 1 potting compost or a peat-based 'multicompost'. Use a funnel made from cardboard to insert the compost into narrow-necked bottles. Plant directly into this.

If your bottle has a narrow neck you'll have to use a little ingenuity, or

A bottle planted up

better still, a spoon attached to the end of a bamboo cane. Scoop out a hole in the compost and drop the plant into place, root-ball first, firming the compost back around it with a cotton reel pushed on the other end of the bamboo cane.

Plant at spacings to allow for growth, and water the compost after planting, taking care not to make a deep reservoir of water in the bottom. Moist, not soggy, is the aim.

Once the miniature crystal palace is planted it needs to be put somewhere where it will be happy. This generally means in good, but indirect light – the sort you can find about three or four feet away from a window. Too much light will lead to scorching of the foliage and rapid drying out of the foliage. Too much shade will lead to slow and spindly growth and loss of foliage colour. Split the difference and the plants will be happy.

As far as feeding goes, apply dilute liquid feed once a month from May to September; that's usually enough to keep these miniatures in good shape.

When the whole thing becomes too much like a jungle for your taste, simply take it apart and start again, preferably in spring when the plants can start to grow away again rapidly.

67

PESTS AND DISEASES

Here they are, the source of all your worries – the beasts and blights that nibble and gnaw, and suck and smother. If you knew how many there are you'd probably give up before you started, but the chances are that you'll never encounter them all, just the commonest types that are a pain in the neck most years.

With the current passion for being 'green' and not racing around blasting sprays at everything there's a tendency to ignore all pests and diseases. Do so if you're happy to have bugs and flies all over your roses and vegetables.

Personally I use very few sprays, and then with great care, so that epidemics are reduced and both my plants and the wildlife in my garden are happy. With a running total of around 43 different species of birds, and four-legged visitors who include deer, foxes, hedgehogs, moles and rabbits I reckon I've got the balance about right. That said, I only use a couple of pesticide sprays: the one I recommend below for greenfly, and a combined pesticide and fungicide on my roses. I apply them in the early evening when bees are in the hive and pets and children are in bed.

Good cultivation, which includes the use of organic fertiliser like blood, bone and fishmeal, and the application of plenty of garden compost and well-rotted manure, means that plants grow vigorously and are less likely to be knocked for six by a pest or disease outbreak.

Here are the commonest pests and diseases you'll be troubled with:

Aphids
Greenfly, blackfly and all shades in between. They suck sap, weaken plants, transmit virus diseases that stunt and distort, and also secrete sticky honeydew on which grows sooty mould. Do you still want to ignore them? A strong squirt with a hose will dislodge them, and very mild washing-up water blocks their breathing pores. ICI 'Rapid Greenfly Killer' (based on pirimicarb) is a specific aphicide which kills the aphids but not bees, ladybirds or lacewings (the last two of which are responsible for devouring a goodly number of garden pests).

Whitefly
Most frequently encountered in greenhouses. A pain because the young stage is not a fly but a sort of scale about as big as a pinhead. The scales are not always affected by spraying, so spraying has to be repeated two or three times at weekly intervals to knock out the emerging flies. Use 'Bio Flydowner'. Whitefly are often seen on fuchsias and plants with soft, downy leaves.

Mealy bug
A pest that covers itself in a mealy white wool. Found mainly in greenhouses and on house plants. Can be bumped off with Murphy 'Tumblebug'.

Brown scale
Tiny brown 'limpets' that cling to stems and the underside of the main leaf veins. Prominent on orange and lemon trees and weeping figs. Dabbing them with a small paintbrush dipped in methylated spirits will kill them. Sponging off is a temporary measure but they soon return. 'Tumblebug' will see them off for longer.

Slugs and snails
The scourge of seedlings and the vegetable plot. Small blue slug pellets can be scattered very thinly – one every

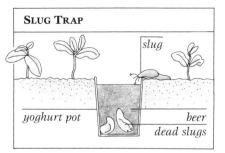

SLUG TRAP

slug

yoghurt pot

beer
dead slugs

3 inches (8 cm) – among susceptible plants. Some argue that these result in poisoned hedgehogs and thrushes but in my garden the poisoned molluscs are never touched by their predators once they are dying. An alternative means of control is to sink empty yoghurt pots into the ground around your plants and to fill the container with beer. The molluscs love the stuff and will fall in and drown. Older methods of leaving half a grapefruit skin turned upside down on the soil can be tried, but this does mean that you'll have to empty the skin every day for the system to be effective.

Mildew and blackspot
The two most prominent diseases of roses. One is black, the other is white. Spray two or three times during the season with ICI 'Roseclear' or pbi 'Multirose'. Both control greenfly as well. Pick up and burn all fallen leaves in autumn to prevent the fungal spores from overwintering. Many varieties have thick leaves that make them less susceptible to attack. Varieties of *Rosa rugosa* are seldom affected.

Ants
A nuisance when they build nests under patios and the roots of plants. Boiling water will reduce their numbers under paving; baits and powders based on borax seem to me to be effective only in the short term. You could try the old method of sprinkling them

with dried and powdered pennyroyal which is said to repel them.

Rabbits
Good wire netting fences sunk into the ground for about 1 foot (30 cm) will help keep them out. Young trees are best protected with spiral plastic rabbit guards. Some plants are more prone to attack than others. Grow those that are left alone and phase out their real favourites.

Rust diseases
Usually evident as orange spots on the undersides of leaves. Can often be controlled by spraying with a copper fungicide.

Honey fungus
Plants in the garden wilt and die for no apparent reason. Dig up some of the roots and you may find black 'boot-laces' and white fungal growth. Clusters of honey-coloured toadstools may erupt in autumn. The fungus is common on privet hedges. There's nothing you can do except dig up and burn affected plants. Manure the soil well and plant something else.

Caterpillars
The leaves and shoots of a wide variety of plants are eaten. Hand pick them if you can bear it and if they are only present in small numbers. Larger infestations can be sprayed with ICI 'Picket' on vegetables and fruits and with Bio 'Flydowner' on ornamental plants.

Red spider mites
You'll have a job to see these little chaps, but they suck the sap on the undersides of plant leaves, turning them yellowish and brittle. Fine webbing can also be seen. A moist atmosphere discourages them in the greenhouse. Spraying them with malathion kills them off for a while, but repeated doses will have to be given.

WEEDS

I remember being told time and time again: 'A weed is any plant growing out of place; a rose can be a weed in the cabbage patch.' I wish that were the case. Most of us are plagued with uglier plants that grow where we don't want them to: bindweed, ground elder, couch grass, dock, dandelion and daisy.

All too often the weeds are allowed to get out of hand and that makes even more work. We were told another old saw: 'One year's seed means seven years' weed.' Get the little blighters out when they're young and their seeds will not have been shed to live another day.

There are several ways of getting rid of weeds.

Annual weeds

These are the ones with thin root systems that do not persist year after year. They are easy to hoe off. Keep your Dutch hoe sharp with a file so that the top growth is severed from the roots and they'll not re-emerge if polished off in a dry spell.

In small places where few weeds are evident, hand weed, pulling out the weeds and consigning them to the compost heap.

Weeds in paths and drives

Easy to keep clean with path and drive weedkillers which are applied with a watering can. They kill existing weed growth and make a barrier in the soil below to stop others emerging. They'll keep a path or drive or patio weed-free for about a year. You can also buy this kind of residual weedkiller for use on rose beds and shrubberies, but I'm not keen on using it there on a regular basis. Better, I reckon, to mulch (see below).

Thick-rooted perennial weeds

These are one of the gardener's biggest problems. Take your pick from ground elder, bindweed, horsetail, oxalis, buttercup, dock, dandelion and couch grass. Couch grass is now less of a problem because it can be controlled, when growing among other plants, by spraying with May & Baker 'Weed-Out' which will kill it but not its neighbours. For best results it should be applied in spring when growth is vigorous.

Most other perennial weeds can be controlled by spraying with Murphy 'Tumbleweed', but this will kill cultivated plants as well as weeds. Horsetail is best bruised by beating it with a

Annual weeds	Perennial weeds
chickweed	bindweed
fat hen	buttercup
groundsel	celandine
annual meadow grass	couch grass
	dandelion
	dock
	ground elder
	horsetail
	oxalis

Horsetail

70

stick before the 'Tumbleweed' is applied; this helps absorption. For details on controlling ground elder et al., in flower beds and borders, see page 46.

Brambles
Woody weeds that I prefer to grub out by hand. Alternatively, SBK 'Brushwood Killer' will help to discourage them.

The use of ground-cover plants
Leaving large gaps between plants just makes work. Plant things closer together and they'll leave less room for weeds to colonise. Some plants form such thick carpets that they make great weed suppressors. Oxalis is a pernicious weed, but its small size makes it easy to smother with thick groundcover plants. Try, for example, *Geranium macrorrhizum* which will soon swamp it.

Geranium macrorrhizum

New ground
When digging a new bed or border I always hand-weed as I go, throwing annual weeds into the bottom of the trench and pulling out the perennials. It's far easier, I think, than spraying or watering on a herbicide.

If you really insist on killing weeds with chemicals, spray the area to be dug at least two months before you tackle it, then you'll be confident that 'Tumbleweed' or whatever has worked.

Never be tempted to use the total weedkiller sodium chlorate. It spreads sideways in the soil and so endangers nearby plants, and it is highly flammable. It also lasts in the soil for around six months.

Mulching
This is a solution so wonderful that it's almost magic. Once you've weeded a bed or border, and planted it up with perennials or shrubs, lay a thick blanket of garden compost, well-rotted manure or pulverised bark on the surface of the moist soil. Make this blanket 3 inches (7–8 cm) thick and it will seal in moisture and keep down weeds. You'll be amazed at the growth rate of the plants, too.

It may seem expensive at the outset (especially if you use bark) but it lasts well. Bark will endure for at least four years if it's not disturbed. Any fertiliser that needs to be applied can simply be scattered on to the surface of the mulch and allowed to be washed down by rain.

Towards the back of deep beds and borders, where the mulch will not be seen and the smart appearance of chipped bark is not essential, straw makes a cheaper substitute.

Before laying any mulch, I always give the ground a dusting of blood, bone and fishmeal so that some goodness is sealed in to give the plants a push in the right direction.

Spring is the best time for mulching – when the soil is moist but warming up.

On the vegetable plot you can even use black polythene as a mulch under strawberries and soft fruits. Hold it in place by burying the edges in the soil. But where a really smart effect is wanted, use an inch-and-a-half (4 cm) of gravel, pea shingle or even small pebbles as a mulch. Odd weeds will push up from time to time but they are easy to pull out by hand.

71

GARDENER'S ALMANAC

All gardeners need a dig in the ribs from time to time. Should I prune my roses now? When's the best time to sow a lawn? Can I plant my bulbs? So here's an at-a-glance calendar to offer gentle reminders. They're not orders, just hints. If you're told that now's the time to plant your bedding, don't do it slavishly if the soil is a sea of mud. Use your own good judgement as well.

JANUARY
Send off your seed order.
Keep off lawns in frosty weather.
Plant rose bushes, trees and shrubs.
Prune fruit trees and bushes.
Spray fruit trees with a tar oil winter wash to kill pests.
Put rabbit guards around stems of young trees if necessary.
Sow exhibition onions in a greenhouse.
Lay turf if weather is mild and dry.
Firm back plants lifted by frost.
Dig over the vegetable plot.
Put plastic netting over winter brassicas to keep off pigeons.
Plant three potatoes in a large flower pot in the greenhouse for an early crop.
Prune wisteria.

Knock snow off evergreens.
Feed birds in cold and frosty weather.
Prune summer-flowering deciduous shrubs.
Melt ice on frozen pools to let fish breathe.

FEBRUARY
Prune roses.
Clip faded flowers from heathers with a pair of shears.
Cut autumn-fruiting raspberry canes down to within 6 inches (15 cm) of the ground.
Prune large-flowered clematis by cutting back to sprouting buds.
Spray outdoor peaches with dithane to control peach leaf curl.
Force rhubarb under buckets of straw outdoors.
Sow bedding plants in a heated greenhouse.
Buy seed potatoes and stand them on a windowsill to sprout.
Plant rhubarb and Jerusalem artichokes.
Prune winter-flowering shrubs after blooming.
Make rock gardens.
Plant lily bulbs.
Sprinkle a little sulphate of ammonia around fruit trees.

FORCING RHUBARB

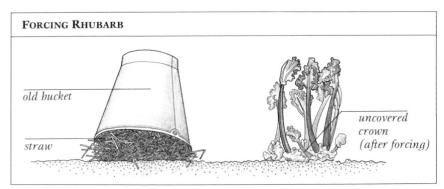

old bucket

straw

uncovered crown (after forcing)

72

Complete digging on the vegetable
plot.
Plant shallots.
Spike lawns to help with surface
drainage.
Pick up any fallen leaves from rose
beds to help control blackspot.
Plant trees and shrubs, fruit trees and
bushes.
Pot up hippeastrum bulbs.
Dig up and divide snowdrops after
flowering.

MARCH
Divide and replant established border
perennials and replant new ones.
Complete pruning of roses.
Lay turf.
Plant lily of the valley.
Plant strawberries.
Complete planting of bare-root trees,
shrubs and roses.
Protect plants from slugs.
Sow bedding plants in a greenhouse.
Scatter rose fertiliser around
established bushes and hoe it in.
Sow sweet peas outdoors.
Mulch raspberries with manure or
garden compost.
Prick out seedlings in the greenhouse.
Repot house plants.
Plant gladioli.
Sow tomatoes, cucumbers and melons
in a greenhouse.
Mulch ground around shrubs and
border plants with bark, well-
rotted compost or manure to keep
down weeds.
Take cuttings from pot plants in a
greenhouse.
Plant alpines and rock-plants.
Prune young plum trees.
Pollinate outdoor peaches.
Sow broad beans, beetroot, broccoli,
Brussels sprouts, cabbages, carrots,
cauliflowers, kale, kohl-rabi, leeks,
lettuces, onions, parsnips, peas,
radishes, spinach and turnips
outdoors.
Plant early potatoes and onion sets.

APRIL
Sow lawns on prepared ground.
Lay turf.
Prune forsythia.
Start to mow lawns.
Plant gladioli.
Plant sweet peas.
Spray with pirimicarb to control
greenfly.
Plant asparagus crowns.
Plant maincrop potatoes.
Sow hardy annual flower seeds
outdoors.

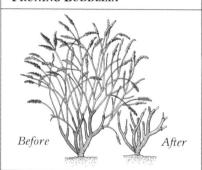

PRUNING BUDDLEIA

Before   *After*

Prune buddleias.
Make garden pools.
Spray gooseberries with benomyl to
control mildew.
Spray roses with 'Multirose' or
'Roseclear' to keep them free of
pests and diseases.
Keep down weeds by hoeing and
hand-pulling.
Repot house plants.
Sow marrows and melons in a
greenhouse.
Take cuttings of pot plants and root
in a propagator.
Plant greenhouse tomatoes.
Stake tall border plants.
Sow vegetables as for March.
Plant out leeks.
Sow runner beans and sweet corn in
individual pots in a greenhouse.
Pot up begonia and gloxinia tubers.

MAY

Feed lawns with a combined weedkiller and fertiliser.
Plant dahlia tubers at the foot of sturdy stakes.
Spray to control greenfly.
Plant up hanging baskets.
Plant water-lilies and aquatic plants.
Spread straw or black polythene around strawberries.
Harvest asparagus.
Sow vegetables as for March, plus French and runner beans and sweetcorn.
Plant out runner beans raised under glass.
Stake peas with brushwood.
Greenhouse shading will be needed from now on.
Stake gladioli.
Harden off bedding plants in a cold frame.
Plant celery.
Feed pot plants once a fortnight from now until October.
Dig up and divide large clumps of polyanthus.
Summer bedding plants can be planted out during the last week of May in the south.
Thin out fruits on gooseberries and use in a pie.

JUNE

Clip hedges.
Plant out bedding in the north.
Hang up hanging baskets.
Water plants and lawns with a sprinkler in dry weather.
Keep a lookout for pests and diseases and act quickly when they are seen.
Protect strawberries from slugs.
Plant tomatoes, runner beans, sweet peppers and marrows outdoors.
Sow vegetables as for March.
Sow wallflowers and other spring bedding plants in rows on the vegetable plot.
Prune shrubs that flowered in May.
Mow regularly.
Shorten the side-shoots on gooseberries.
Plant melons in garden frames.
Stop harvesting asparagus.
Take cuttings of pot plants.
When overcrowded clumps of large-flowered irises finish flowering, dig them up, divide them and replant in fresh ground.
Protect raspberry fruits from birds by covering with plastic netting.
Cut down the leaves of daffodils and narcissi growing in the garden.

SUMMER PRUNING OF GOOSEBERRIES

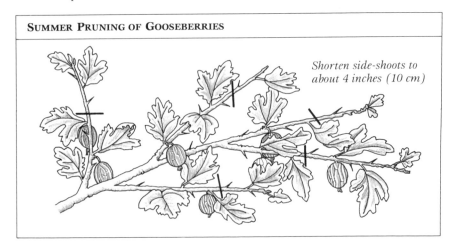

Shorten side-shoots to about 4 inches (10 cm)

PLANTING LEEKS

Hole is dibbed in 4 inches (10 cm) deep; plant is dropped in and puddled in

JULY

Shorten long shoots on wisteria to about a foot (30 cm).
Dead-head roses and border plants.
Water hanging baskets, window-boxes and pot plants regularly.
Cut back strawberry plants and remove straw after harvesting.
Plant leeks and winter cabbage.
Sow broad beans, beetroot, carrots, endive, kohl rabi, lettuce, radish, spinach, Swiss chard and turnips.
Peg down strawberry runners to propagate new plants.
Take cuttings of pot plants.
Take cuttings of carnations and pinks.
Summer prune trained apple trees.
Transplant wallflowers and spring bedding plants to a wider spacing.
Scatter rose fertiliser around bushes and hoe it in.
Cut and dry herbs for winter use.
Plant madonna lilies.
Plant new strawberry beds.
Order fruit trees and bushes for autumn planting.

AUGUST

Plant autumn crocuses and colchicums.
Dead-head roses and border plants.
Clip yew hedges and topiary specimens.
Plant corms of hardy cyclamen.
Cut out raspberry canes at ground level when they finish fruiting, and tie in new canes.
Plant strawberries.
Bend over onion tops to ripen bulbs.
Mulch runner beans with grass clippings.
Take cuttings of pot plants.
Pot up freesia corms for winter flowers.
Make sure newly planted shrubs and trees do not dry out.
Cut and dry everlasting flowers.
Take cuttings from garden shrubs and root in a propagator.
Sow spring cabbage, endive, kohl rabi, lettuce, radish, spinach and turnips.
Spot treat lawns to control weeds.
Prune rambling roses when flowers fade.
Pick early apples as they ripen.
Hoe between vegetable rows to keep down weeds.
Set the blades of the lawn mower higher in dry weather.
Make a new compost heap.

75

SEPTEMBER

Sow lawns.

Plant spring-flowering bulbs outdoors where they are to flower.

Root 1-foot (30-cm) long cuttings of rose shoots outdoors. Make them pencil-thick and bury them for two thirds of their length.

Tie in new raspberry canes to the support wires.

Harvest plums and damsons.

Plant spring cabbages.

Cut and dry herbs for winter.

Dry off onions under cloches or in a greenhouse.

Sow lettuce, spinach and turnips.

Take cuttings of pelargoniums.

Sow hardy annuals outdoors where they are to flower next summer.

Plant lily bulbs.

Pull out faded hardy annuals.

Lay turf.

Take cuttings of conifers and root in a propagator.

Prepare ground for fruit trees and bushes to be planted in autumn.

ROSE CUTTINGS

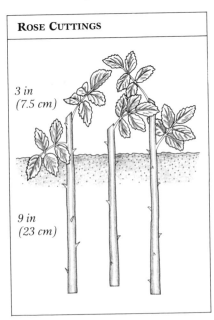

3 in
(7.5 cm)

9 in
(23 cm)

Pot up rooted cuttings.

Plant evergreens lifted from open ground.

Remove unripened fruit from outdoor tomatoes and ripen it indoors.

Cut out blackberry canes that have finished cropping.

Dig up and store potatoes, carrots and beetroots.

Sow cauliflowers and lettuce.

OCTOBER

Pull up summer bedding plants as they fade.

Plant spring bulbs in pots and keep cool and dark for eight weeks.

Dig up, dry off and store gladiolus corms.

Plant wallflowers and other spring bedding plants.

Plant spring-flowering bulbs in the garden.

Lay turf.

Scarify lawns with a wire-tooth rake and spike them to improve drainage.

Plant conifers and evergreens.

Pick and store apples and pears.

Box up a few mint roots to provide leaves in a greenhouse in winter.

Take hardwood cuttings of deciduous shrubs and root them outdoors.

Plant border perennials.

Dig up and store dahlia tubers when frost blackens the leaves.

Tie in stems of wall-trained fruit trees and snip off any that are not wanted.

Remove greenhouse shading.

Check that tree ties are not too tight.

Sweep up and stack fallen leaves.

Cut down and clear away asparagus foliage.

Mow much less regularly, with blades set higher.

Sow 'Aquadulce' broad beans in a sheltered spot.

Start to dig the vegetable plot.

NOVEMBER

Plant trees, shrubs, fruit trees and bushes dug up from the nursery.
Dig manure into vacant ground in beds, borders and vegetable plot.
Plant new hedges.
If trees and shrubs arrive when the ground is not fit for planting, lay their roots in a temporary trench and cover them with soil.
Continue to sweep and stack fallen leaves.
Pot up rooted cuttings.
Stop feeding house plants, and water them more carefully.
Snip faded flower stalks off roses to reduce their height.
Lay turf.
Prune fruit trees.
Keep geraniums very much on the dry side.
Send the mower off for servicing.
Send for seed catalogues.
Plant spring-flowering bulbs in the garden.
Cut down faded border plants.
Snip dead twigs off shrubs.

DECEMBER

Check that all raspberry canes are tied in and spaced out on their supports.
Melt ice on garden ponds to let fish breathe.
Plant bare-root trees and shrubs.
Feed garden birds in cold weather.
Pick faded flowers and leaves off greenhouse plants.
Pot up hippeastrum bulbs.
Bring pot-grown hyacinths and narcissi indoors.
Plant border perennials.
Keep off lawns in frosty weather.
Knock snow from evergreens.
Check fruit in store and throw out any that are rotting.
Prune greenhouse grape vines.
Winter-wash fruit trees.

HEELING IN

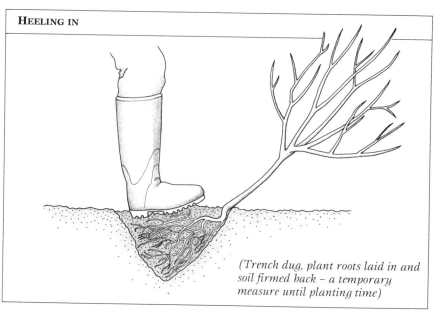

(Trench dug, plant roots laid in and soil firmed back – a temporary measure until planting time)

INDEX

Page numbers in *italic* refer to the illustrations